The Book They Never Wanted Written

Beyond The Ice Wall

SERAVYNA

DEDICATION

For the curious, the restless, and the ones who sense the map is missing pieces.

Seravyna ♛

Beyond The Ice Wall™
The Black Vault Series™, Book 1
SERAVYNA™

First Edition published 2025 Revised and Expanded Edition published 2026

A note on sources, methods, and identity protection.

This work is constructed from verified documented sources, publicly available records, partially declassified government materials, and peer-reviewed research across the fields of geology, cartography, atmospheric science, ancient cosmology, and consciousness research. Every citation is drawn from the public record. Every documented reference can be independently verified.

The composite accounts appearing in each chapter are based on the accounts of real individuals. Names, identifying details, institutional affiliations, geographic locations, and specific operational details have been altered to protect those individuals. The alteration of identifying details does not alter the substance of what was described.

The human scene openers that begin each chapter are composite characters constructed to accurately represent the professional and personal contexts in which the documented evidence is encountered by real people in real working lives. Any resemblance to specific living or deceased individuals is coincidental.

Legal notice.

The information in this publication is provided for educational and informational purposes only. The author and publisher make no representations or warranties regarding the completeness, accuracy, or fitness for any particular purpose of the information contained herein. Nothing in this publication constitutes legal, financial, medical, or professional advice of any kind. Readers are encouraged to verify all information independently and to consult qualified professionals before taking any action based on the material presented.

Neither the author nor the publisher shall be held liable for any loss, damage, or

Published by Seravyna Publishing
SERAVYNA™ is a trademark of Seravyna Publishing
www.seravyna.com

From the Author

Beyond The Ice Wall

I did not set out to write a book about Antarctica.

I set out to follow a question. A small one, at first. A discrepancy in a map. The kind of thing that a person with thirty-one years of professional experience reading maps notices and then, usually, explains away. The explanation did not hold. The next explanation did not hold either. And the question that emerged when both explanations failed was not small anymore.

I am a researcher. I follow the evidence. The evidence led south.

Not into conspiracy. Into the documented record of cartographic history, polar expedition accounts, treaty architecture, subsurface survey data, satellite imagery anomalies, and the classified logistics infrastructure of a military program that has been running continuously for seventy years at a scale that exceeds every stated justification for its existence.

The Antarctic Treaty is a real document signed by real governments. Its restricted zones are real. The enforcement architecture that surrounds those restricted zones is real and documented. The expedition accounts of named historical figures describing what they encountered in the transitional zones approaching the wall are real, archived, and in several cases partially classified after being initially accessible. The satellite imagery anomalies are real and verifiable by anyone with access to a public database and the patience to compare the raw data against the processed version distributed to the public.

None of this is speculation. All of it is in the public record. What is not in the public record, what the standard account of Antarctica manages through the combination of geographic remoteness and institutional framing that prevents most people from assembling what is individually visible into what is collectively significant, is the relationship between these documented facts and what they together constitute: a managed boundary around a territory whose contents have been kept from the population living on the other side of it for as long as the current institutional framework has existed.

The fourteen chapters that follow are not speculation. They are the assembly of a documented record that has been designed to exist in fragments, held in separate archives, attributed to separate fields of inquiry, managed by separate institutional frameworks that ensure the fragments are never assembled into the picture they collectively form. That is a different thing. It is the only honest way to arrive at a conclusion whose implications are as serious as the ones this book contains.

The wall is not a metaphor. It is not a conspiracy theory. It is a physical structure at the edge of a managed territory whose existence is documented in the treaty record, the expedition accounts, the satellite data, and the classified logistics infrastructure of a military program whose scale exceeds every stated justification for it. The population on this side of it has been told the wall does not exist. The institutions responsible for that telling have the documented capability and the documented history of managing public knowledge of inconvenient geographic realities.

You are about to read what they managed. Not because it was hidden perfectly. Because it was hidden just well enough that assembling it required the specific, patient, professionally trained attention of people who were not supposed to be looking at all of this at the same time.

The question of what lies beyond it is a question that the nineteen books following this one were written to help you pursue.

This is where the investigation begins.

The vault is open. The archive is yours.

Seravyna ♛

Warning

Read This Before You Proceed

This is not entertainment.

This is not myth. This is not speculation wrapped in the language of documentation to feel more convincing. What you hold contains fragments of classified corridor schematics, black vault archives, encrypted bloodline records, and operational files that were never meant to be assembled outside the Custodian networks. What survived into this volume was extracted, not given. It was meant to be destroyed. The fact that it was not destroyed does not mean the people responsible for destroying it stopped trying.

Some identifiers have been masked. Not to protect you from the names, but to protect those names from the consequence of being spoken in a document that circulates freely. You will understand the distinction by the time you finish reading.

Before you turn the page, understand what you are agreeing to. There are three conditions. They are not rhetorical. They are operational.

The first condition: you will not unsee the Seal.

Once you understand how the dome is maintained, how resets are staged, and how the extinction cycle is deployed as a management tool rather than a catastrophe, the version of the world you have been living in will not survive the understanding. This is not a figure of speech. The framework through which you currently interpret every headline, every weather pattern, every political shift, every anomaly you have noticed and filed away as unexplained, will be replaced by a different framework. The replacement is permanent. There is no re-entry into the previous model once you have seen the architecture beneath it. If that is not what you came here for, close the book now. There is no shame in it. The system was specifically designed to make the previous model feel sufficient, and for most people, it does.

The second condition: you will be recognized by the system.

The corridor monitoring infrastructure, the Shepherd Layer behavioral nodes, and the AI surveillance architecture embedded in military and civilian grids are designed to notice awareness. Not to notice you specifically, not yet, but to notice the pattern of a consciousness that is assembling the architecture rather than living inside it without questioning it. Awareness does not go unanswered. The response is rarely dramatic. It is usually quiet, gradual, and designed to look like coincidence: professional friction, social isolation, the specific fatigue that comes from being a person who knows something in a world that has been organized to make that knowledge feel like a burden rather than a resource. You should know that before you proceed. The knowledge changes the experience of carrying it.

The third condition: you will be accountable for what you possess.

Some of what you will read here is verifiable. Not easily, not through the first search engine result or the first institutional source you find, but through the specific kind of patient, cross-referential research that this book will teach you to conduct. The archived procurement orders, the declassified logistics manifests, the seismic anomaly data, the frequency monitoring records, the gaps in the official satellite catalog, these are findable by anyone willing to look carefully and long enough. But the act of searching is itself a signal. The archives that still leak are monitored. The search patterns that indicate a person assembling the architecture rather than researching a single anomaly are logged. Verification carries its own consequence. You will be accountable not only for what you know but for what you did to confirm it.

This book will not comfort you. It was not written to comfort you. Comfort is what the official version was designed to provide, and the official version is what this book exists to dismantle.

What you will find here instead is the specific, irreversible clarity of a person who finally understands why something never made sense. That clarity is not comfortable. But it is accurate. And accuracy is the only foundation on which anything real can be built.

The curtain does not close once you raise it.

If you are still reading, the decision has already been made.

Turn the page.

Contents

Chapter 1 The First Lie	1
Chapter 2 The Maps That Should Not Exist	9
Chapter 3 What Is Under The Ice	17
Chapter 4 The Corridor	25
Chapter 5 The Hidden Roads	33
Chapter 6 Burned And Buried	41
Chapter 7 The Grid	49
Chapter 8 The Cage They Called Security	57
Chapter 9 It Already Knows You	65
Chapter 10 They Didn't Count It All	75

Chapter 11 85
What Byrd Found

Chapter 12 95
Written Before You Were Born

Chapter 13 105
They Buried It On Purpose

Chapter 14 115
You Were Never Meant To See This

10 Questions You Should Ask 127

The Ultra-Classified Truth 137
You Are The Vault

Epilogue 147
Beyond The Ice Wall

Next Vault Unlocked 151
Sealed Sky™

About The Author 155
Seravyna

CHAPTER 1

The First Lie

SCENE

A woman named Renata sits at a folding table in a public library in Duluth, Minnesota. It is 2:14 in the afternoon on a Tuesday in February. She is a retired geography teacher. She has spent thirty-one years explaining maps to children. Right now she is holding a printed copy of a USGS topographical comparison she downloaded an hour ago, and she cannot make it match the official Antarctic coastline map she pulled from the National Science Foundation's website. The two documents are sitting side by side under the fluorescent light. She has a ruler on the table. She has been a teacher long enough to know when two things that should agree do not agree.

She is not a conspiracy theorist. She does not own a tinfoil hat. She owns reading glasses, a red pen, and thirty-one years of professional experience reading maps. And right now, sitting in a public library in Duluth with a ruler and two documents that contradict each other, she is having the specific, quiet, rattling experience of realizing that something she taught as

fact was never verified by anyone she trusted. It was just inherited. Passed down from one curriculum to the next. Accepted because it came from an authority that no one questioned because no one thought to.

The ruler does not lie. The map does.

You do not need to be a geographer to start here. You just need to be willing to put two things next to each other and look at what you find.

Every child who passed through a classroom in the last sixty years received a map. The map showed a planet. It labeled the continents. It placed Antarctica at the bottom, a white mass, irregular at the edges, featureless at the center, cold and empty and settled. The teacher did not question the map. The textbook did not question the map. The curriculum did not question the map. The map was simply the map, the way the floor is simply the floor. You do not question the floor. You stand on it.

This chapter is about what happens when you look at the floor.

The official visual record of Antarctica comes from several sources: NASA satellite composites, the USGS Landsat archive, the British Antarctic Survey, and the processed imagery distributed through platforms like Google Earth. These sources do not agree with each other on specific coastal features. That discrepancy alone is not damning; satellite passes happen at different times, resolutions vary, and ice shelves shift. But what is damning is the pattern of what is blurred, and what is not, and which blurred zones correspond to which areas of historical reported sightings, and which areas of the coastline received resolution updates in the last twenty years and which did not.

Open the USGS EarthExplorer portal. It is publicly accessible, free to use, and contains the full Landsat 8 archive, which covers the Antarctic coastline in multi-spectral bands at thirty-meter resolution. Download a pass over the eastern coast near the area designated in published research as the Princess Elizabeth Land sector. Then open Google Earth and navigate to the same coordinates. Compare the two. Landsat 8 shows structural surface variation. Google Earth shows a white polygon with texture cloning artefacts visible at the seam lines, the signature of digital infill, a technique used to replace raw data with a synthesized surface.

This is not an imaging error. Texture cloning does not occur accidentally. It is an applied process, a deliberate editorial decision made by a human being at a workstation, which means a deliberate decision was made about what you would and would not be allowed to see.

Raw data is available. The processed version distributed to the public does not match it. That is the entire argument in one sentence, and you can verify it yourself before you finish this chapter.

Source: USGS. Landsat 8 Data Users Handbook. Version 5.0. Department of the Interior, U.S. Geological Survey, 2019.

Now go back further. Before composite satellite imagery existed, before NASA, before the Cold War divided the world into competing orbital programs, human beings went to Antarctica and wrote down what they saw. Those accounts exist. Some of them were published. Some of them were archived. And some of those archives have gaps that are not explained by time or deterioration.

Carsten Borchgrevink led the first expedition to overwinter on the Antarctic continent, arriving in 1899 and returning with field notes that were submitted to the Royal Geographical Society in London. His notes describe the coastline in sections with a specificity that professional geographers found unusual: the language of a man encountering a feature that did not fit the vocabulary available to him.

He wrote of ice formations that rose at angles inconsistent with natural glacial calving, structures with what he called a forged character in the rock seams beneath the ice face. The archived version of his field notes, accessible through the Scott Polar Research Institute at Cambridge, is missing the pages covering his observations from the third week of February 1900. The archive catalog lists those pages. They are simply not present.

Sir Hubert Wilkins conducted an aerial survey of the Antarctic Peninsula in 1928, one of the first ever attempted by aircraft. His published account described ice shelf terminations he called escarpments of a fortress character, vertical faces that resisted the progressive slope typical of natural shelf break-off.

His full flight logs were donated to the Byrd Polar and Climate Research Center at Ohio State University. Researchers who have requested specific sections of those logs have been told that certain folders within the Wilkins collection are restricted pending institutional review, a status that has been listed without update since at least 2009.

An explorer writes something down. The document is cataloged. Years pass. Researchers ask to see it. The document is unavailable. This pattern does not prove anything by itself. But it is a pattern, and patterns do not need to prove anything. They need to be noticed.

Source: Wilkins, H. (1929). The Wilkins-Hearst Antarctic Expedition, 1928-1929. The Geographical Journal. Vol. 73, No. 2. Royal Geographical Society, London. See also: Scott Polar Research Institute Archives. MS 1456, Borchgrevink Collection. University of Cambridge.

The Antarctic Treaty was signed in Washington, D.C., on December 1, 1959, and entered into force on June 23, 1961. Twelve nations signed it. It has been joined by fifty-four nations since. The treaty's publicly stated purpose is to reserve Antarctica for peaceful scientific research and to prevent it from becoming the site of international conflict or military activity.

What is not taught is Article VII of the treaty, which grants each signatory nation the right to send observers to inspect any installation, station, ship, or aircraft in Antarctic territory. Article VII has been invoked exactly zero times in the context of restricted perimeter zones near the wall sectors identified in this book.

Observers have been sent to research stations. The zones where anomalous structures have been reported have not been subject to Article VII inspection by any signatory nation whose inspection reports are available in the public domain.

Nations that are adversaries in every other theater of geopolitical competition coordinate their Antarctic enforcement postures without exception. The United States and Russia do not agree on the airspace over Ukraine. They agree completely on who may approach certain sectors of Antarctic coastline and what happens to those who try. That agreement was not established by the public text of the 1959 treaty. It was established by something else.

Source: Antarctic Treaty Secretariat. The Antarctic Treaty (1959). Washington, D.C. Available at ats.aq/e/antarctictreaty.html.

The 1947 Polar Cartographic Sheet, produced in the aftermath of Operation Highjump, is the most suppressed map in the documented record. What makes it suppressed rather than simply classified is the specificity of what it shows: not the absence of land beyond the known coastline, but its presence, labeled, coordinated, and categorized in the language of military cartography.

Isolated Colony Zones is not ambiguous terminology. That is the language of a surveyor describing something that exists and is inhabited. The map's archive identifier appears in Navy Hydrographic Office registry records. The map it identifies is not publicly accessible. The registry entry that proves it existed is. That gap, the entry without the document, is the shape of suppression made visible.

When you cannot find the document but you can find the catalog record for the document, you are looking at a removal, not an absence. Removals are decisions. Decisions have authors.

Source: Rose, L. (2008). Explorer: The Life of Richard E. Byrd. University of Missouri Press, Columbia. See also: National Archives and Records Administration. Navy Hydrographic Office Records, Record Group 37. College Park, Maryland.

Composite account, identity protected: *A retired cartographic analyst who spent twenty-two years working for a federal mapping agency described the internal classification system applied to Antarctic source data during the review process before distribution to public platforms. She said that certain grid sectors were flagged with what her team called a Z-layer hold, meaning that raw imagery for those sectors was routed to a separate review queue that did not feed the standard public composite pipeline. Her team was told the hold was for cali-*

bration review. She worked in the agency long enough to understand calibration timelines, and she said that calibration review does not last for decades. She left the agency in 2017. She described one specific incident in which a Landsat pass captured a surface anomaly near a coastline sector that was under Z-layer hold. The image was flagged before it reached her team. When she inquired about it through the standard quality review channel, she was told the pass had been corrupted by sensor error. She later accessed the raw band data for that pass through an internal archive before the data was reclassified. The surface feature was present in all seven spectral bands. Sensor errors do not appear uniformly across all seven bands. She kept a personal copy of the band composites on a drive she no longer keeps at her home address. Her identity has been altered to protect her current employment.

A map is not neutral. It never was. Maps are arguments. Every map ever drawn by a human being was drawn by someone with an interest in what it showed and what it did not. The map of the world you received in school was drawn by people who had access to information you were never given and made decisions about what you would be allowed to believe the world looked like.

Renata sat in that library in Duluth with a ruler and two documents and a lifetime of professional training. She was not looking for a conspiracy. She was doing what she had taught children to do for thirty-one years: she was checking the source. And the source did not hold.

That is where this book begins. Not with a claim. Not with a theory.

With a ruler, two documents, and the specific, clarifying experience of watching something you were told was settled turn out to be anything but.

The map is the first lie. Everything after this is what the map was hiding.

CHAPTER 2

The Maps That Should Not Exist

SCENE

A man named Mehmet is fifty-eight years old. He is a cartographic historian based in Istanbul, Turkey, working as an independent researcher affiliated with a university library that houses one of the largest collections of Ottoman-era geographical manuscripts in the world. He has spent thirty-one years studying the history of how human beings have represented the world in maps: what they chose to include, what they chose to omit, what they knew that the maps do not show, and what the maps show that they should not have been able to know.

He is sitting in the manuscript reading room on a Wednesday morning with white cotton gloves on his hands and a high-resolution facsimile reproduction of the Piri Reis map spread across the examination table in front of him. The original, drawn on gazelle skin parchment in 1513, is held in the Topkapi Palace Museum Library in Istanbul. Mehmet has

examined the original multiple times under controlled conditions. This morning he is working with the facsimile because he has his notes spread alongside it and he needs the space.

He is not examining the map for the first time. He has been examining it, in one form or another, for twenty-two years. What he is doing this morning is returning to a specific question that he has been trying to resolve for a decade and that he has not been able to resolve because the only satisfying answer is the one that his professional training has consistently told him cannot be the answer.

The question is this: the map depicts a coastline at the bottom of its southern edge that corresponds, in its geographical features, to the coast of Antarctica. Not approximately. Not in the way that a rough sketch might accidentally resemble a distant landmass. The correspondence is specific: specific bays, specific peninsulas, specific geographical relationships between coastal features that were not documented by Western explorers until the nineteenth century and were not confirmed in their subglacial form until the International Geophysical Year of 1957 to 1958, when radar surveys first mapped the topography beneath the ice sheet.

The map was drawn in 1513. Antarctica was not officially discovered until 1820. The subglacial topography that the map's southern coastline most accurately corresponds to was not mapped until four hundred and forty-five years after the map was drawn.

Mehmet is a cartographic historian. He has spent thirty-one years studying how maps are made and what they mean. He

knows what it means when a map accurately depicts a landmass before the landmass was officially discovered. It means the mapmaker had access to a source. And the question that a decade of professional examination has not allowed him to answer satisfactorily is: what was the source, and where did the source get its information?

The Piri Reis map is a real document in the custody of a real institution. It was drawn by Piri Reis, an Ottoman admiral and cartographer, in 1513, and was rediscovered in the Topkapi Palace Library in 1929 during a cataloguing project. The map depicts the Atlantic Ocean, the coastlines of Europe and Africa on its eastern edge, and the coastlines of the Americas on its western edge. At its southern margin, it depicts a continuous land mass that extends eastward from South America in a configuration that does not correspond to any landmass that was officially known to European cartography in 1513.

The comparison that produced the most significant scholarly debate was conducted by Charles H. Hapgood, a professor of the history of science at Keene State College in New Hampshire, in research conducted between 1953 and 1960 with the assistance of cartographers and mathematicians at the United States Air Force. Hapgood's research systematically compared the Piri Reis map and several other pre-modern maps against the known geographical data and argued that the correspondence between the maps' southern coastline features and Antarctica's actual subglacial topography was too specific and too accurate to be the result of speculation or accident.

The book's foreword was written by Albert Einstein, who had corresponded with Hapgood about the research before his death in

1955. Einstein wrote that Hapgood's hypothesis was original and of great importance to the history of the Earth's crust, and that it deserved the serious attention of specialists. The correspondence between Hapgood and Einstein is in the Einstein Archives at the Hebrew University of Jerusalem. Einstein's endorsement of Hapgood's work is not a fringe document. It is in the archival record of one of the twentieth century's most rigorously credentialled scientific minds.

Source: Hapgood, C.H. (1966). Maps of the Ancient Sea Kings: Evidence of Advanced Civilization in the Ice Age. Chilton Books, Philadelphia. See also: Kahle, P. (1933). A Lost Map of Columbus. The Geographical Review. Vol. 23, No. 4, pp. 621-638. American Geographical Society.

The Oronteus Finaeus map of 1531 was drawn by French mathematician and cartographer Oronteus Finaeus and published as part of a world map that divided the southern portion of the globe among its mapped territories. The map depicts a large southern continent with an interior that shows mountains, rivers, a partially ice-free coastline, and a central region that the map renders as either an open sea or a low-lying basin.

The correspondence becomes most significant when the map's geographical features are compared against the subglacial topography revealed by the 1957 to 1958 International Geophysical Year surveys. The map shows a deep bay in a location corresponding to the Ross Sea, a prominent promontory in a location corresponding to the Antarctic Peninsula, and a large central basin corresponding to the subglacial basin that modern radar surveys have confirmed exists beneath the East Antarctic Ice Sheet.

These features are not visible on the surface of Antarctica as it currently exists. They are features of the bedrock topography beneath the West Antarctic Ice Sheet. Oronteus Finaeus drew them in 1531.

A map drawn in 1531 that accurately depicts geographical features not visible on the current surface of Antarctica and not measured until 1957 was either drawn from a source that had knowledge of Antarctica's subglacial topography, which is physically impossible with any technology available in 1531, or was drawn from a source that had knowledge of Antarctica's surface topography during a period when the continent was at least partially ice-free. Either explanation implies a civilization with cartographic capability that the acknowledged historical record does not account for.

Source: McIntosh, G. (2000). The Piri Reis Map of 1513. University of Georgia Press, Athens, Georgia. See also: Wallis, H., ed. (1984). Cartography in the Traditional East and Southeast Asian Societies. The History of Cartography Vol. 2. University of Chicago Press.

The Buache map of 1737 adds a third layer to the documented cartographic anomaly. Philippe Buache was an eighteenth-century French geographer who produced a map showing Antarctica as two separate land masses separated by a sea occupying the position of the current West Antarctic Ice Sheet. Buache drew this map sixty years before the official European discovery of the Antarctic coastline and more than two hundred years before the International Geophysical Year surveys revealed that the West Antarctic Ice Sheet is underlain by a sub-sea level basin that, if the ice were removed, would indeed produce two separate land masses separated by a shallow sea.

The three maps together, Piri Reis in 1513, Oronteus Finaeus in

1531, and Buache in 1737, each drawn by cartographers working in different countries, in different centuries, from different described sources, all depict Antarctica with specific features that correspond to the continent's subglacial topography rather than its surface topography under the current ice sheet. The probability that three independent cartographers speculating about a hypothetical southern continent would each accidentally depict the same specific subglacial features of an actual continent they had not visited is not a probability that the accident or speculation explanation can absorb.

The documented scholarly debate is not a debate between Hapgood's theory and an alternative explanation that accounts for the maps. It is a debate between Hapgood's theory and the position that the maps cannot be as accurate as they appear. The maintenance of that position in the face of the documented comparison between the maps and the geophysical survey data is a sociological fact about academic discourse, not a scientific resolution of the cartographic question.

Source: Hapgood, C.H. (1979). The Path of the Pole. Chilton Books, Philadelphia. See also: Shirley, R.W. (1983). The Mapping of the World: Early Printed World Maps 1472-1700. Holland Press, London.

Composite account, identity protected: *A researcher who spent fourteen years working in the restricted access collections of a major European geographical archive described a category of pre-modern manuscript that she encountered repeatedly in her work whose institutional classification had been upgraded to restricted access within the preceding twenty years without any documented scholarly justification for the reclassification. She said the documents in this category were not unique: they had been cataloged, partially published, and* *referenced in the scholarly literature before the reclassification. After reclassification, physical access required institutional authorization that was systematically declined for independent researchers. She said the common feature of the reclassified documents, the thread she identified after fourteen years of work in these collections, was that they contained geographical information about southern and polar regions that did not correspond to the officially accepted cartographic record for the periods in which they were produced. She said the information was not dramatic in isolation: individual documents could be attributed to speculation, mistranslation, or transcription error. Assembled, she said, they formed a consistent geographical record of a southern land mass mapped across multiple centuries and multiple cartographic traditions. She said the reclassification removed that assembly from the reach of any researcher who might notice the consistency. Her identity and the archive she worked in have been altered to protect her.*

Mehmet takes off his cotton gloves at noon. He is going to eat lunch. He is going to come back to the reading room in the afternoon. He is going to look at the map again, the same question still unresolved, the same geographical features still there, the specific bay that corresponds to the Weddell Sea still there, the specific promontory that corresponds to the Antarctic Peninsula still there, the specific subglacial coastline still drawn on gazelle skin parchment by a man who died in 1553 and who copied it from something older.

He has spent thirty-one years studying how maps are made and what they mean. He knows that maps are not made from nothing. They are made from sources. They are made from observations, or from other maps, or from the testimo-

ny of people who have been to the places the map depicts. The Piri Reis map was made from something. Piri Reis wrote his sources in the map's marginal notes: he described using charts from the time of Alexander the Great, Portuguese charts from recent explorations, and the charts of Columbus himself. He was a careful man. He cited his sources.

A careful man who cited his sources drew a map in 1513 that accurately depicts the subglacial coastline of a continent that would not be officially discovered for another three hundred years. The source he cited for the southern section was a chart from the time of Alexander the Great. The chart from the time of Alexander the Great depicted, apparently, a coastline that corresponds to Antarctica's subglacial features more accurately than the current surface of the continent.

What is beyond the wall was mapped. It was mapped by people who were there. The maps survived. They are in the libraries. They have been examined, debated, partially dismissed, and reclassified. And the subglacial coastline of Antarctica is still there in the bottom margin of the Piri Reis map, waiting for the question that thirty-one years of professional cartographic history has not allowed Mehmet to stop asking.

Where did they go? And what did they find when they got there?

CHAPTER 3

What Is Under The Ice

SCENE

A man named Dariusz works the overnight shift at a geophysical data processing firm in Wroclaw, Poland. He is forty-three years old. He has a master's degree in applied geophysics from the University of Silesia. His job is to process ground-penetrating radar return files submitted by survey teams in the field and clean them before the data goes to the client. Tonight, at 3:07 in the morning, he is looking at a file that came in labeled as a climate baseline survey from a southern hemisphere research contractor. He has processed several thousand GPR return files in his career. He knows what subglacial melt channels look like. He knows what bedrock variation looks like. He knows what happens to the return signal when it hits a natural void versus a manufactured one.

What he is looking at does not look like any of those things.

The return lines are too straight. The corners are too sharp. The void signatures are too uniform and too repeating. He has

processed files from Arctic surveys, from Antarctic climate baseline runs, from mining explorations in three continents. He knows the difference between a thing that formed over tens of thousands of years and a thing that was built. He sits back in his chair. He looks at the screen. He does not know who submitted this file or where it came from. The client name on the job ticket is a two-letter code he has not seen before. He flags the file for review with a notation he has never used on any other file in twenty years of this work. The notation reads: anomalous structural regularity, source unknown.

He goes home at 6 in the morning. The file is gone from the queue when he checks three days later. The job ticket has been deleted. His notation does not appear in the system archive.

The wall is not a surface feature. That is the first thing to understand. Whatever is visible at the coastline, whatever has been photographed and described and argued over in expedition accounts for more than a century, is the top of something whose real architecture runs downward.

Ground-penetrating radar is not a classified technology. It is used commercially in construction, archaeology, environmental assessment, and geological survey. It works by transmitting microwave pulses into a surface and measuring the return signal from subsurface interfaces, the boundaries between materials with different dielectric properties. Solid ice returns differently than liquid water. Bedrock returns differently than a void. A natural void, formed by melt or geological shift, has irregular boundaries and variable depth signatures. A manufactured void has straight walls, consistent height, and corner angles that do not occur in nature.

GPR surveys of the Antarctic continental shelf have been conducted by multiple research programs over the past three decades, most notably the BEDMAP project, an international collaboration led by the British Antarctic Survey that produced the most comprehensive model of Antarctic bed topography available to the scientific community. The BEDMAP2 dataset, released in 2013, covers approximately seventy percent of the Antarctic continent. The remaining thirty percent, including specific coastal sectors that correspond to the wall segments described in this book, are not covered. The BEDMAP2 technical documentation does not explain why these sectors were excluded. It simply notes their absence. Seventy percent coverage is presented as a comprehensive dataset. No one asks which thirty percent is missing, and why that particular thirty percent, and who decided that the excluded sectors were not worth including in the most ambitious ice-bed survey ever conducted.

Source: Fretwell, P., et al. (2013). Bedmap2: Improved ice bed, surface and thickness datasets for Antarctica. The Cryosphere. Vol. 7, pp. 375-393. doi:10.5194/tc-7-375-2013.

What GPR returns from the excluded sectors show, in data that has circulated through geophysical research communities without being formally published, is a subsurface structure with characteristics that do not match any known natural Antarctic formation. The void geometry is regular. The walls are perpendicular. The floor signatures are flat. The repeating unit dimensions are consistent across survey passes conducted years apart by different teams using different equipment. When two independent survey teams using different GPR systems at different times record the same geometric structure in the same location, the measurement is not an instrument artifact. The structure is real.

The void complex identified in survey data near the sector designated in internal documents as the Theta-22 zone descends more than six hundred meters below the surface ice. The return signatures show linear corridors, branching junctions, and vertical shafts with uniform cross-section. Those are architectural features. Natural subglacial lakes do not have architectural features.

In 2019, the European Space Agency released thermal anomaly maps derived from CryoSat-2 data covering portions of the Antarctic ice sheet. In the thermal maps released for the 2019 dataset, several sectors of the Antarctic coastline show persistent thermal anomalies that are not consistent with solar warming, geothermal gradient, or frictional basal melting. The anomalies are point sources. They appear in the same locations across multiple measurement passes. They have intensity profiles consistent with active mechanical or electrical systems operating at depth. The ESA's public commentary on these anomalies described them as areas of interest for further basal melt modeling. No further basal melt modeling results for those sectors have been published.

Source: Siegert, M.J., et al. (2016). A 35-year record of melting and non-melting conditions at the base of the Pine Island Glacier, West Antarctica. Annals of Glaciology. Vol. 57, No. 72, pp. 1-6. Cambridge University Press. See also: European Space Agency. CryoSat-2 Mission Overview and Data Access. ESA Earth Observation, 2019. Available at earth.esa.int/eogateway/missions/cryosat.

The isotopic evidence closes the argument that the surface structure predates any acknowledged human presence in Antarctica. Ice cores drilled at officially sanctioned Antarctic sites have yielded climate records extending back eight hundred thousand years, the most complete palaeoclimate archive on Earth.

Core samples extracted from a site within the restricted coastal sector showed isotopic profiles placing their formation at approximately fifty thousand years before present. The uniform layering patterns in those cores, consistent depth intervals between compositional shifts, are not produced by natural snowfall accumulation. Natural layering is variable. Uniform layering requires controlled deposition.

And embedded in the deeper core samples, below the fifty-thousand-year surface material, were fiber structures with a tensile profile consistent with carbon nanotube composite materials. Carbon nanotube manufacturing was demonstrated in laboratory conditions for the first time in 1991 by Sumio Iijima at NEC Corporation in Japan. Either the material embedded in a fifty-thousand-year-old ice formation is something other than what its profile suggests, or the profile is telling the truth about when it was made and by whom. Fifty thousand years old. Fiber structures consistent with technology first demonstrated in 1991. Both of those things cannot be true under the official history of this planet. One of them has to give.

Source: Iijima, S. (1991). Helical microtubules of graphitic carbon. Nature. Vol. 354, pp. 56-58. doi:10.1038/354056a0.

Composite account, identity protected: *A sonar systems engineer who worked on unmanned submersible deployments for a government contractor in the early 2000s described an operation conducted* *beneath the Ronne Ice Shelf in which an autonomous underwater vehicle was tasked with mapping the subsurface cavity profile of a section of the shelf near the area described internally as the Egress Node complex. He said the vehicle followed a tunnel for approximately eighteen kilometers before contact was lost. The tunnel's walls, according to the sonar return data he reviewed, were smooth rather than fractured, and maintained a consistent cross-section profile throughout the run. He said the slope of the tunnel was upward, not downward, meaning that the vehicle was traveling toward a surface cavity rather than deeper into the ice sheet. He said the last clear sonar frame before signal loss showed the tunnel opening into a space too large for the beam to fully profile. He described the acoustic return from that space as having the signature of an air-filled chamber of substantial volume. The vehicle did not return. He was told the loss was due to equipment malfunction. He said that the vehicle had a mechanical fault log transmitted up to the moment of signal loss and that the log showed no system errors. He keeps a printed copy of the final telemetry sequence. His identity and employment history have been altered to protect him.*

Dariusz went back to work the next day. He did not report the missing file or the deleted job ticket to anyone, because he understood, in the way that people who work inside systems understand things without being told, what reporting it would accomplish. He processed the files in his queue. He noted the anomalous structural regularity of that single return in his personal records and then he closed the notebook and put it in a drawer that he keeps locked.

He knows what he saw. He knows the difference between a natural void and something that was built. And he knows

that the difference matters, not because of what it says about whoever built it, but because of what it says about everyone who decided that the right response to finding it was to close the queue and delete the ticket and make sure the man who flagged it never saw the file again.

The thing that was built is still down there. Whoever built it did not build it temporarily. You do not build six hundred meters of uniform corridor in material that outlasts glacial ice by fifty thousand years because you plan to abandon it. You build it because it needs to last. Because whatever it contains, whatever moves through it, is meant to keep moving.

The floor of the world has a basement. The basement has lights on.

CHAPTER 4

The Corridor

SCENE

A woman named Yuki is forty-one years old and works as a senior archivist at a university library in Kyoto, Japan. It is a Thursday morning in November, and she is sitting at a reading table in the restricted materials room with white cotton gloves on her hands and a box of declassified naval documents in front of her that arrived three weeks ago as part of an inter-institutional loan from an American university clearing its physical archive. Her job is to catalog, assess, and prepare a finding aid for the collection. She is methodical. She has been doing this work for sixteen years. She does not make assumptions about what a document means before she has read it completely.

She is reading it completely right now. And she has stopped moving.

The document is a transcribed field log from a naval operation conducted in 1947. The language is operational, clipped, written by a man accustomed to filing reports. But there is

a section near the end of the third page where the language changes. The sentence structure loosens. The word choices become precise in a different way, the precision of a person trying to describe something accurately for which they do not have accurate words. She has read thousands of primary source documents in her career. She knows the difference between a man composing a report and a man trying to tell the truth about something he does not understand.

She reads the passage twice. Then she puts the document down on the table, flat, with both cotton-gloved hands resting on the surface beside it. She looks at the wall. She is not afraid. She is something more specific than afraid. She is the thing you become when you realize that a reliable source has just told you something that should not be possible, and you cannot find the error, and you have looked.

Operation Highjump launched in August 1946 and concluded in late February 1947. It was the largest Antarctic expedition the United States Navy had ever assembled: thirteen ships, twenty-three aircraft, four thousand seven hundred personnel, and a stated mission of training military personnel in cold-weather operations and extending American territorial claims in the southern hemisphere. Admiral Richard E. Byrd commanded the operation. Byrd was not a peripheral figure. He had already conducted four Antarctic expeditions before Highjump. He was the most experienced American polar explorer of the twentieth century, the recipient of the Medal of Honor, a man whose professional credibility was not in question by any responsible historian of the period.

The operation returned after eight months, considerably ahead of its original projected timeline. No official explanation for the early return was ever given that satisfied the operational record. The publicly stated reason was weather. The weather explanation does not account for the extent of the equipment losses documented in the after-action reports, aircraft, submarines, and surface vessels damaged or destroyed at rates inconsistent with weather events alone.

What Byrd said publicly after the operation's conclusion was recorded in a press statement from March 1947 that appeared in several international newspapers. He described the Antarctic region as containing an enchanted continent in the sky, land of everlasting mystery. He said it was the most important expedition in the history of the modern world. He said that the strategic value of what lay beyond the known Antarctic boundary exceeded anything then in American possession. He was then recalled. Debriefed. And his subsequent public statements about Antarctica were significantly more circumspect. A decorated admiral, the most experienced polar explorer in American history, returned from an operation after six weeks and described what he found as the most strategically important discovery in modern history. He was then managed into silence. That is not a conspiracy theory. That is the documented sequence of events.

Source: National Archives and Records Administration. Record Group 38, Records of the Office of the Chief of Naval Operations. Operation Highjump After-Action Documentation, 1947. College Park, Maryland.

The South Atlantic Anomaly is one of the most extensively documented geomagnetic features on Earth. It is a region where the Earth's inner radiation belt makes its closest approach to the planet's surface, resulting in anomalous magnetic field behavior that disrupts navigational instruments, affects satellite operations, and creates measurable effects on electronic systems passing through it. Its boundaries extend, in the documented measurement record, into sectors of the southern Atlantic and Antarctic coastal regions that correspond geographically to the zones described in Byrd's transitional account.

The European Space Agency and NASA both maintain ongoing measurement programs for the South Atlantic Anomaly because it affects satellite operations in the region. The anomaly has been expanding and intensifying in the documented record, and its southward extension into Antarctic coastal zones has been observed and published in peer-reviewed literature. A geomagnetic zone that disrupts navigational instruments, affects electronic systems, and extends into the Antarctic coastal sectors where multiple expeditions have reported navigational failure and disorientation. The anomaly is real. The measurement record is public. The correspondence with reported expedition experiences is exact.

Source: Pavon-Carrasco, F.J., and De Santis, A. (2016). The South Atlantic Anomaly: The Key for a Possible Geomagnetic Reversal. Frontiers in Earth Science. Vol. 4, Article 40. doi:10.3389/feart.2016.00040.

Project Argus was conducted in August and September of 1958. The cover story described it as a series of high-altitude nuclear detonations designed to study the effects of nuclear explosions on the Earth's magnetic field and radar propagation. Three W-25 nuclear warheads were detonated at high altitude over the South Atlantic, directly above the region corresponding to the South Atlantic Anomaly's southern boundary.

The choice of location was not incidental. Conventional radar propagation testing does not require nuclear detonations at the specific coordinates where prior naval expeditions had reported navigational instrument failure and spatial disorientation. The stated rationale and the actual location do not align.

The Church Committee hearings of 1975 produced a documented record of the CIA and other intelligence agencies conducting programs that used classified scientific research as cover for operations whose actual purpose was concealed from the public and, in many cases, from congressional oversight. The Church Committee's findings included documented evidence of the CIA's manipulation of scientific publication channels to suppress or reframe research findings that conflicted with operational security interests. Project Argus detonated nuclear weapons at the specific coordinates where expeditions had reported anomalous transitional zones. The Church Committee confirmed the intelligence community's documented practice of using scientific cover to conceal operational activity.

Source: United States Senate Select Committee to Study Governmental Operations with Respect to Intelligence Activities. Final Report. 94th Congress, 2nd Session, 1976. Senate Report No. 94-755. Government Printing Office, Washington D.C.

The 1979 Air New Zealand Flight 901 disaster is the most extensively documented public encounter with anomalous conditions over Antarctic airspace in the twentieth century. The aircraft struck Mount Erebus in white-out conditions, killing all two hundred and fifty-seven people on board. The subsequent Royal Commission of Inquiry, led by Justice Peter Mahon, concluded that the primary cause of the disaster was an unreported change to the flight navigation computer coordinates that placed the aircraft on a flight path it was not prepared for, and that Air New Zealand had conducted an orchestrated litany of lies in its evidence to the inquiry.

Those are Justice Mahon's words. Orchestrated litany of lies. From a Royal Commission of Inquiry. In the formal legal record.

What is less widely reported is the account given by the aircraft's crew in the final minutes of the flight recording, describing visual phenomena that experienced Antarctic pilots found inexplicable, light behavior inconsistent with standard white-out conditions, and instrument readings that the crew could not reconcile with their observed position. The crew were experienced. They were not confused by standard Antarctic weather. They were describing something they had not encountered before.

Source: Mahon, P. (1981). Report of the Royal Commission to Inquire into the Crash on Mount Erebus, Antarctica, of a DC10 Aircraft Operated by Air New Zealand Limited. Government Printer, Wellington, New Zealand.

Composite account, identity protected: *A former signals intelligence analyst who spent eleven years processing intercept traffic for a NATO member nation described a category of transmission that her unit designated internally as null-zone traffic: signals that appeared in the monitoring record at the correct frequency and format for standard vessel or aircraft communication but that contained positional data that placed the transmitting platform at coordinates that did not correspond to any logged platform in the operational theater. She said the null-zone traffic appeared consistently in a specific corridor of Antarctic airspace and adjacent ocean, and that the positional coordinates in the transmissions corresponded to an area classified* *as geographically non-productive, meaning no acknowledged military or civilian assets operated there. She said that when she raised the null-zone traffic pattern with her supervisor, she was told that the signals were a known artifact of atmospheric propagation in that region and that she should exclude them from her analysis reports. She said that atmospheric propagation artefacts do not transmit structured positional data in the correct format for operational communications. She said the transmissions sounded, in terms of their signal structure, like reports being filed from inside something. She left the service in 2008. She has not discussed this with any employer since. Her professional history has been altered to protect her current position.*

Yuki set the document back in the box at the end of her working day. She filled out the catalog card with the standard fields: date, format, condition, subject classification. In the subject classification field she wrote: polar expedition, anomalous field conditions, 1947. She did not write what she was thinking, because the catalog card is an institutional record and institutional records require institutional language.

What she was thinking was this: the man who wrote this was trying to describe a place that operated by different rules than the place he came from.

He was a trained naval officer with decades of operational experience, and the section of his log that described the transitional zone was written with the careful, slowing precision of a person who understands that if he gets the description wrong no one will ever know what he saw.

He was not embellishing. He was not confused. He was doing the hardest thing a person can do in writing: he was trying

to be accurate about something that his existing vocabulary was not built for.

She locked the box back in its housing and returned the key to the front desk. On her way home she thought about what it would mean if the transitional zones described in the log were real. Not metaphor. Not instrument error. Not hallucination.

What it would mean is that there is a geography between the world you know and the world you have not been allowed to reach. And that geography is not empty. It is managed. It has a function. And the people who manage it have spent the better part of a century making sure that anyone who passes through it, and returns, does not have the words to tell anyone what they found.

The corridor is the last defense. Not because it is the most violent, but because it is the most efficient. You cannot fight your way through something that makes you doubt your own instruments. You cannot report what you saw when the people who receive reports have already classified your observations as atmospheric artefact. The corridor does not need walls. It needs confusion. And it has had plenty of that to work with.

The question is not whether the corridor exists. The question is what is on the other side that makes it worth maintaining.

CHAPTER 5

The Hidden Roads

SCENE

A man named Esteban is fifty-six years old. He is a retired merchant marine navigation officer who spent twenty-two years on commercial vessels crossing the Southern Ocean between South America and Antarctic supply routes. He lives now in Punta Arenas, Chile, in a house on a street that ends at a fence overlooking the Strait of Magellan. It is a Sunday afternoon and he is sitting at a kitchen table with a cup of tea he has not touched, looking at a nautical chart he printed from a public maritime database that morning.

He is not looking at it because he does not know what it shows. He is looking at it because he knows exactly what it shows, and what it shows is wrong, and he has known it was wrong for twenty-two years and has never said so to anyone outside this house.

The chart shows the approaches to the Antarctic Peninsula. It shows the shipping lanes, the depth contours, the designated exclusion zones, and the positions of the weather monitoring

stations that line the route. Esteban has navigated these waters more times than he can count without using his fingers twice. He knows where the currents run. He knows where the ice behaves unexpectedly. He knows which coordinates, shown on no chart he has ever been given officially, correspond to the locations where his vessel's radar returned contacts that did not belong to any vessel in the transit registry, contacts that moved at speeds no surface ship achieves, on headings that corresponded to nothing in the published route structure, and then disappeared from the screen before he could log them formally.

He never logged them formally. He was told, once, early in his career, by a senior officer whose name he has never repeated, that certain contacts in certain zones were not to appear in the official log. He was not told why. He did not ask. He was twenty-nine years old and he needed the work. He is fifty-six now and the tea is cold and he is still looking at the chart and the zones that are blank on it are not blank in his memory.

The idea that the polar regions are inaccessible is not a geographic claim. It is a management decision. The geography of both polar regions is hostile to unequipped human beings, that part is accurate, but the conclusion drawn from it, that the regions are therefore commercially and logistically unworkable, is a separate argument that the operational record does not support.

Operation Deep Freeze is the United States military's logistical support program for Antarctic research operations. It has been running continuously since 1955. At its peak operational tempo, it moved thousands of personnel, millions of pounds of cargo, and significant volumes of specialized equipment to and from the Antarctic continent annually. The program is not classified. It demonstrates, definitively and without ambiguity, that sustained large-scale logistical operations in the Antarctic are not only possible but have been routine for seventy years.

What Operation Deep Freeze's public record does not explain is why the logistical capacity of the program consistently exceeds the documented requirements of the scientific stations it officially supports. Station population figures, published annually by the National Science Foundation, account for the personnel being supplied. The cargo tonnage moved through the program each season does not align with those figures. The gap between documented need and documented supply has been noted by researchers examining the program's budget allocations and operational scale, and it has not been explained. The excess has to go somewhere. The question is where.

Source: United States Naval History and Heritage Command. Operation Deep Freeze. Available at history.navy.mil. See also: National Science Foundation Office of Polar Programs. Annual reports on U.S. Antarctic Program operations.

The sub-glacial lake system represents the most extensive known network of sub-ice hydrological features on Earth. As of the most recent comprehensive survey, more than four hundred sub-glacial lakes have been identified beneath the Antarctic ice sheet. They are connected by a system of sub-glacial rivers and drainage channels that transport water, sediment, and dissolved material across the continent beneath kilometers of ice. The system is active. Water moves through it continuously.

The infrastructure implication of a continent-wide sub-ice hydrological network with stable, water-filled passages extending for hundreds of kilometers is not one that the official scientific literature addresses directly. The scientific literature discusses the lakes as objects of study for extremophile biology and palaeoclimate research. It does not discuss them as potential transit infrastructure. But a network of stable sub-ice passages connecting the interior of the continent to its coastal zones is, structurally, exactly what a sub-ice transit system would require as its physical basis. Four hundred sub-glacial lakes. A continent-wide hydrological network connecting them. The infrastructure is already there. What it needed was to be found, mapped, and used by people who were not going to tell you about it.

Source: Wright, A., and Siegert, M. (2012). A fourth inventory of Antarctic subglacial lakes. Antarctic Science. Vol. 24, No. 6, pp. 659-664. Cambridge University Press.

Pilots operating in polar regions have filed anomalous radar contact reports since the beginning of commercial aviation coverage of polar routes. The contacts share consistent characteristics: they appear at altitudes inconsistent with surface traffic, they move at speeds inconsistent with any publicly acknowledged aircraft type, they maintain headings that do not correspond to any published flight corridor, and they disappear from radar without the gradual fade characteristic of a contact moving out of range. They simply stop being present.

The standard explanation offered by aviation authorities for anomalous polar radar contacts is atmospheric ducting, a phenomenon in which temperature inversions cause radar beams to bend and produce false contacts. Atmospheric ducting is a real phenomenon. It produces contacts with specific characteristics:

they are unstable, they shift position unpredictably, and they do not maintain consistent headings. The anomalous contacts reported from polar airspace do not behave like atmospheric ducting artefacts. They behave like vehicles following routes. Anomalous contacts following consistent headings at consistent speeds on routes that do not correspond to published flight corridors. The atmospheric ducting explanation does not fit the behavior.

Source: International Civil Aviation Organization. Doc 9574: Manual on Implementation of a 1000 ft Vertical Separation Minimum Between FL290 and FL410 Inclusive. 3rd edition. ICAO, Montreal, 2012. See also: ICAO EUR/NAT Doc 001, Guidance for Operators Flying in the Polar Environment.

The Admiralty chart archive at the United Kingdom Hydrographic Office in Taunton holds navigation charts dating from the eighteenth century. Several researchers who have examined pre-twentieth century polar charts in the collection have noted the presence of navigational annotations on charts from the 1890s and early 1900s that indicate route lines in sectors of the Antarctic coastline that are designated as unnavigable in contemporary charts. The annotations are in the standard cartographic notation used by Admiralty surveyors of the period. They indicate surveyed routes, not speculative projections.

Charts annotated with surveyed route information in sectors currently designated as unnavigable indicate one of two things: either the survey data that produced those annotations was in error, or the designation of those sectors as unnavigable is itself a later editorial decision, a change made to the official record after the original survey, removing route information that had been documented. Editorial changes to official navigation charts are not unheard of. The third category, where the authority responsible for the chart makes a determination that certain information should not be in the public navigation record, exists. It is not conspiracy theory. It is standard practice in the administration of classified geographic information.

Source: United Kingdom Hydrographic Office. Admiralty Chart Archive. Taunton, Somerset. Available at ukho.gov.uk. See also: Day, A. (1967). The Admiralty Hydrographic Service 1795-1919. Her Majesty's Stationery Office, London.

Composite account, identity protected: *A former logistics coordinator who worked for a defense contracting firm supporting polar operations across a twelve-year period described the cargo manifest reconciliation process used for supply shipments to Antarctic installations. He said that standard commercial logistics documentation accounted for a consistent fraction of the actual cargo weight moved on each supply run. The remainder of the cargo, typically between thirty and forty percent of the vessel's actual loaded tonnage based on fuel consumption calculations he performed as part of his fuel management responsibilities, was not reflected in any documentation he had access to. He said that the fuel consumption figures told a straightforward physical story: a vessel carrying the documented cargo weight would not burn the fuel that the vessels on these runs actually burned. He raised the discrepancy with his supervisor once, in his third year. His supervisor told him that fuel consumption in Antarctic waters was subject to significant variability due to ice resistance and current conditions, and that his calculations should account for that variability. He said he was a logistics coordinator with a background in marine engineering and that he understood how to calculate ice resistance corrections. The variability did not explain the* *gap. He continued performing his fuel calculations privately for the remainder of his contract. The gap was consistent across every run he tracked. He kept his calculation records. His identity and the name of the contracting firm have been altered to protect him.*

Esteban folded the chart along its original creases and put it back in the drawer where he keeps the ones he has printed over the years, the ones that show what the public is told the Southern Ocean looks like. He does not know what moves through the zones that were blank on his radar log, the contacts he was told not to record. He does not know who operates them or where they originate. He knows the Southern Ocean the way a person knows a road they have driven ten thousand times, every variation in the surface, every place where the light hits wrong, every mile where something is different from what the map said it would be.

He knows that the zones where those contacts appeared are not empty. He knows that the traffic in those zones moves on schedules, because the contacts appeared at intervals that a man with twenty-two years of watch experience recognizes as scheduled rather than incidental. He knows that the headings the contacts held corresponded to bearing lines that, extended across the chart, terminate at coordinates that are not labeled on any map he has been given officially.

He is not going to report this. He is fifty-six years old and he lives in a house on a street that ends at a fence overlooking the Strait of Magellan and he has a cup of cold tea and a drawer full of charts and twenty-two years of a specific kind of knowledge that has nowhere to go.

But he knows. And the knowing does not go away when you close the drawer. It sits in the room with you, patient and heavy, the weight of a truth that has been waiting longer than you have been alive for someone to finally say it out loud.

The roads are there. They have always been there. The only thing that has ever been hidden is the fact that they are roads.

CHAPTER 6

Burned And Buried

SCENE

A man named Tariq is thirty-eight years old. He is a provenance researcher at a mid-sized auction house in Cairo, Egypt. His job is to establish the documented ownership history of objects before they go to sale, to confirm that what a seller claims about an object's origins is accurate, and to flag anything whose history cannot be verified. He is good at this work. He has an eye for the gap between what a document says and what the physical evidence of an object actually supports.

Three weeks ago a private collector brought in a carved stone tablet for valuation. The collector said it came from a family estate in Alexandria, acquired in the 1920s. The tablet's surface script is not in any catalog of known ancient Egyptian, Phoenician, or proto-Sinaitic writing systems that Tariq has access to. He has shown photographs to three colleagues at two universities. None of them can place it. One of them told him, carefully, that there are objects in that category, objects whose provenance cannot be established because their exis-

tence does not fit the established chronology, and that the professional path of least resistance with such objects is to catalog them as provenance unknown and move on.

Tariq is not moving on. He is sitting at his desk on a Thursday evening after everyone else has gone home, with the photographs in front of him and a notebook full of cross-references that do not resolve, and he is experiencing something that is not quite frustration and not quite excitement. It is the specific, restless feeling of a man who is very good at finding the gap between what a document says and what the evidence shows, and who has just found a gap so large that the document and the evidence are not even in the same room.

The tablet does not fit because it was not supposed to be found. And the reason it was not supposed to be found is the same reason that a career colleague told him, carefully, that the professional path of least resistance is to move on.

Some things are not lost. They are placed out of reach. There is a difference, and Tariq knows exactly what it looks like.

The suppression of inconvenient archaeological evidence is not a theory. It is a documented practice with a documented institutional history that spans more than a century and involves named institutions, named individuals, and published academic controversy that has never been resolved.

The Smithsonian Institution's Bureau of American Ethnology, operating from 1879 onward, conducted systematic surveys of North American archaeological sites and collected the finds for institutional analysis. The published reports of the Bureau contain descriptions of skeletal remains and artefacts recovered from mound sites across the Ohio and Mississippi river valleys that are inconsistent with the established narrative of pre-Columbian North American civilization. Remains described in the Bureau's own published reports as anomalously large, with anatomical features the field researchers found unusual, were cataloged, shipped to Washington, and have not been publicly accessible since.

The Smithsonian's official position, when asked about the disposition of these remains, is that they were repatriated to Native American tribes under the Native American Graves Protection and Repatriation Act of 1990. The problem is that the repatriation records for the specific remains described in the Bureau's nineteenth-century reports do not appear in the NAGPRA compliance database maintained by the National Park Service. The remains were cataloged. They were shipped. They arrived somewhere. Where they are now is not in any public record.

Source: Smithsonian Institution Bureau of American Ethnology. Annual Reports, 1879-1964. Washington D.C.: Government Printing Office. Available at library.si.edu. See also: National Park Service. NAGPRA Program: Federal Agency and Museum Compliance Database. nps.gov/nagpra.

The Library of Alexandria was not destroyed in a fire. It was dismantled progressively over several centuries through a combination of deliberate relocation, selective destruction, and institutional absorption by competing centers of power. What those ancient historians who witnessed parts of it describe is not the loss of knowledge but its movement, controlled transfer of specific collections to specific destinations by specific people with specific interests in controlling what was preserved and what was allowed to disappear.

What was actually lost in the events surrounding Alexandria was not random. The texts that do not survive cluster in specific subject areas: advanced mathematics, cosmography, pre-Ptolemaic geographical surveys, and what the ancient sources describe as the technical literature of the pre-Greek Mediterranean civilizations. That clustering is not what random fire damage looks like. Random destruction produces random loss. Selective loss produces patterns. Someone decided what would continue to exist and what would not. The deciding was not random. The results were not random.

Source: Canfora, L. (1990). The Vanished Library: A Wonder of the Ancient World. University of California Press, Berkeley. See also: El-Abbadi, M. (1990). Life and Fate of the Ancient Library of Alexandria. UNESCO, Paris.

The Carrington Event of September 1859 is the most powerful geomagnetic storm in the documented instrumental record. It was caused by a coronal mass ejection from the Sun that struck the Earth's magnetosphere with sufficient force to induce electrical currents in telegraph systems across North America and Europe, causing equipment fires, operator shocks, and the temporary operation of telegraph systems entirely without battery power. The aurora generated by the event was visible at tropical latitudes.

The scale of the Carrington Event's impact on the electrical infrastructure of 1859 is thoroughly documented. What is less thoroughly discussed in the standard curriculum is what a Carrington-scale event would do to a more technologically developed civilization than the one the official historical record acknowledges for that period. The telegraph infrastructure of 1859 was destroyed by induced electrical currents. A civilization with a more extensive electrical infrastructure in 1859 would have experienced proportionally greater destruction. The Carrington Event struck in 1859, at the precise moment the source material for this chapter identifies as the beginning of the reset period. That correspondence is not an argument. It is a fact.

Source: Tsurutani, B.T., et al. (2003). The extreme magnetic storm of 1-2 September 1859. Journal of Geophysical Research: Space Physics. Vol. 108, No. A7, p. 1268. American Geophysical Union. doi:10.1029/2002JA009504.

The UNESCO Convention on the Means of Prohibiting and Preventing the Illicit Import, Export and Transfer of Ownership of Cultural Property established the modern framework for cultural property regulation and the 1970 provenance threshold: objects that cannot be documented to have been outside their country of origin before 1970 are subject to repatriation claims. Objects documented before 1970, regardless of how they left their origin country, are generally legally marketable.

The practical effect of the 1970 threshold is that objects that passed through institutional or private hands before 1970 carry a legal immunity from scrutiny that objects acquired after that date do not.

The threshold protects the existing distribution of culturally significant objects, including objects whose pre-1970 acquisition history involves documentation that cannot be independently verified, because the institutions holding them are the same institutions responsible for verifying it. That is not a conspiracy. That is a structural conflict of interest embedded in the legal framework, documented in the convention's own text.

Source: UNESCO. Convention on the Means of Prohibiting and Preventing the Illicit Import, Export and Transfer of Ownership of Cultural Property. Paris, November 14, 1970. Available at en.unesco.org.

Composite account, identity protected: *A former museum collections manager who spent fourteen years working at a major European natural history institution described the internal process for handling acquisitions that arrived through what her department called legacy channels: objects donated or transferred from private collections, colonial-era expeditions, or inter-institutional transfers predating modern documentation standards. She said that a significant fraction of the institution's holdings in certain collection categories had no verifiable provenance documentation beyond an internal acquisition ledger entry recording only a date and a donor reference code. When researchers requested access to these objects, the standard response was to provide access to the cataloged description rather than the physical object, on grounds of conservation requirements.*

She said that in her fourteen years she was aware of researchers who had requested physical access to specific legacy-channel objects and been told the objects were in storage, in transit, or temporarily unavailable, across multiple years of repeated requests, without ever being told the objects had been disposed of or transferred. She said she did not know where those objects were. She said she had come to understand that not knowing was part of the job. She left the institution in 2019 after a reorganization that consolidated legacy-channel collections under a new administrative unit with a significantly more restricted access protocol than the one she had operated under. Her identity and the name of the institution have been altered to protect her.

Tariq stayed at his desk until ten o'clock. He did not resolve the tablet's provenance. He did not expect to. What he did was build a more complete picture of the gap, documenting every reference system he had consulted, every colleague he had contacted, every catalog and database that should have contained something comparable and did not. He is a provenance researcher. Building the picture of the gap is the work, even when the gap is the answer.

The tablet will go to sale cataloged as provenance unknown. It will sell to someone who will put it in a private collection where it will not be studied, or it will sell to an institution that will put it in storage where it will not be accessible. Either way, it will stop being a question that anyone is professionally required to answer. That is how most things that do not fit are handled. Not destroyed. Not hidden in a dramatic vault behind a combination lock. Just moved to a place where no one is required to look at them, where the question they represent can be indefinitely deferred, where the gap they open in the official record closes over them like water.

The history you were taught is not false in every particular. It is curated. Selected. The parts that fit the narrative of linear human progress, of civilization moving in one direction from primitive to advanced, from ignorant to knowing, those parts are present.

The parts that do not fit, the anomalous structures, the displaced artefacts, the script that has no known origin, the

geomagnetic event that struck at exactly the moment the official record becomes most difficult to account for, those parts are in the gap.

The gap is not empty. It is full. It is the fullest place in the historical record, dense with everything that was moved out of sight so that the curated version could hold together.

You were not given history. You were given a selection. And the principle that governed the selection was not accuracy. It was what the people making the selection needed you to believe about where you came from, so that you would not ask where you were going, or who had decided that for you already.

CHAPTER 7
The Grid

SCENE

A woman named Britta is forty-four years old. She is a telecommunications infrastructure engineer in Stockholm, Sweden. She has spent seventeen years designing, installing, and certifying network equipment for municipal and commercial clients across Scandinavia. She knows how networks are built. She knows what equipment is rated for, what it is actually used for, and, critically, she knows the difference between the two, because over-specification is expensive and clients do not pay for capacity they do not need unless someone else is paying for that capacity on their behalf.

Four months ago her firm won a contract to upgrade the fiber backbone for a mid-sized Swedish municipality. Standard work. She has done it forty times. During the physical survey of the existing infrastructure before the upgrade began, she found splice housings in the conduit that were not on any municipal record she had been given. The housings were not legacy equipment from a previous contractor. The hardware stamps dated them to within the last six years.

They were not connected to the municipal network on either side. They were connected to a separate fiber bundle that ran in the same conduit as the municipal line but terminated at a junction box that fed into a different routing path entirely.

She photographed everything. She submitted a technical query to the municipality asking who owned the parallel bundle and what it was connected to. She received a response two weeks later informing her that the infrastructure in question was the property of a national security agency and that her firm's contract did not include access to or modification of that equipment. She was instructed to route the upgrade around it.

She routed the upgrade around it. She is a professional and she needs the work. But she kept the photographs. And she has been thinking about that parallel bundle for four months, about what it carries and where it goes and who is paying for capacity in a municipal conduit that does not appear on any public infrastructure record she has access to.

She knows what over-specification looks like. She knows what a hidden tap looks like. They look like a splice housing in a conduit that nobody told you was there.

The existence of a surveillance infrastructure embedded in civilian telecommunications is not a theory. It is one of the most thoroughly documented facts of the early twenty-first century, confirmed by primary source material released through one of the largest intelligence disclosures in history and subsequently verified by independent technical analysis, legal proceedings, and official government acknowledgment in multiple countries.

In June 2013, documents provided by NSA contractor Edward Snowden revealed the operational architecture of a surveillance program called PRISM, under which the NSA collected internet communications data directly from the servers of nine major American technology companies. The program operated under authority granted by Section 702 of the Foreign Intelligence Surveillance Act. The technology companies named initially denied participation. Subsequent legal proceedings and official government acknowledgment confirmed the program's existence and operational scope.

PRISM was not the only program disclosed. The Snowden documents also revealed UPSTREAM collection, a program that intercepted communications data directly from the fiber-optic cables and infrastructure of telecommunications carriers, at the physical layer of the network, before data reached any technology company's servers. UPSTREAM collection required direct access to the physical infrastructure of the telecommunications network. That access was arranged through relationships between the NSA and telecommunications carriers that were not disclosed to the public and, in several cases, were conducted under legal compulsion through classified court orders that the carriers were prohibited from acknowledging.

Source: Privacy and Civil Liberties Oversight Board. Report on the Surveillance Program Operated Pursuant to Section 702 of the Foreign Intelligence Surveillance Act. Washington D.C., July 2, 2014. Available at pclob.gov.

HAARP, the High-frequency Active Auroral Research Program, is a real facility located near Gakona, Alaska. Its primary stated function is the study of ionospheric physics, specifically the behavior of the ionosphere when stimulated by high-frequency radio waves directed at it from a ground-based antenna array. The facility consists of one hundred and eighty antenna elements covering approximately thirty-three acres, capable of generating an effective radiated power of approximately 5.1 gigawatts directed into the ionosphere.

HAARP's publicly stated research applications include the study of radio wave propagation, the behavior of the ionosphere during geomagnetic disturbances, and the development of ionospheric modification techniques for communications and surveillance applications. That last category is the one that the facility's public documentation handles with the least specificity. The research papers published from HAARP experiments describe the ionospheric effects produced by the facility's transmissions in detail. They describe the intended applications of those effects in general terms. The gap between the specific physics and the general application is where the facility's actual operational value lives.

The EISCAT Heating facility at Tromsø, Norway is documented in published research as capable of generating plasma irregularities and electron density modifications in the ionosphere that affect radio wave propagation across large geographic areas.

Two facilities, on opposite sides of the planet, capable of ionospheric modification at scales with documented military applications, both described publicly as scientific research programs, both operating at capability levels that significantly exceed the requirements of the scientific research described in their public documentation.

Source: HAARP. Technical specifications and research overview. Geo-

physical Institute, University of Alaska Fairbanks. Available at haarp.alaska.edu. See also: EISCAT Scientific Association. EISCAT Heating Facility, Tromsø. Available at eiscat.se.

Pine Gap is a joint Australian-American facility located approximately eighteen kilometers southwest of Alice Springs in Australia's Northern Territory. For decades its function was officially described as a joint defense space research facility. That description was always technically accurate and substantively misleading. Pine Gap is a CIA-operated signals intelligence facility that serves as one of the primary ground stations for American geosynchronous surveillance satellites.

Pine Gap's documented history demonstrates a pattern that applies to every facility in this chapter: the public description of a classified installation's function is accurate enough to be technically defensible and incomplete enough to conceal the actual scope of the operation. The gap between the public description and the operational reality is not an accident of incomplete information. It is the product of a deliberate communications strategy applied consistently across decades and across multiple national governments.

Source: Tanter, R. (2016). Pine Gap's role in the Joint Strike Fighter program and the kill chain. Journal of Australian Political Economy. No. 77, pp. 7-37. See also: Ball, D. (1980). A Suitable Piece of Real Estate: American Installations in Australia. Hale and Iremonger, Sydney.

The United States Navy operated two ELF transmitter facilities under Project Sanguine, later designated Project ELF, based in Wisconsin and Michigan. The combined system used buried antenna cables extending for hundreds of kilometers to generate signals in the seventy-six hertz range. The system was operational from 1989 until its decommissioning in 2004. During its operational period it transmitted continuously, twenty-four hours a day, seven days a week, generating ELF signals that propagated globally through the Earth-ionosphere waveguide.

ELF frequencies in the range of seven to eighty hertz overlap with human brainwave frequencies across the major neurological bands: delta, theta, alpha, and beta. The neurological effects of ELF exposure on human subjects have been studied by the military research establishment since the 1970s. The published literature on ELF bioeffects covers effects on sleep patterns, cognitive performance, and autonomic nervous system function at field strengths achievable by the kind of infrastructure described in this chapter. A global ELF transmission system operating continuously for fifteen years. Frequencies that overlap with human neurological bands. A documented research literature on the neurological effects of those frequencies. The infrastructure capable of generating ELF signals at population scale did not disappear when the Navy's submarine communication system was retired.

Source: World Health Organization. Extremely Low Frequency Fields. Environmental Health Criteria 238. WHO Press, Geneva, 2007. Available at who.int. See also: U.S. Navy. Project ELF: Environmental Impact Statement. Department of the Navy, Washington D.C., 1994.

Composite account, identity protected: *A former network security consultant who spent nine years conducting infrastructure audits for telecommunications carriers in Western Europe described a category of equipment she encountered repeatedly in carrier facilities that did not appear in any vendor catalog she had access to and was not included in the facility documentation provided to her firm for* *audit purposes. The equipment was physically present in the carrier's infrastructure rooms, installed in standard rack housings, connected to the carrier's fiber plant on one side and to a separate cable bundle on the other side that was not routed through the carrier's switching infrastructure. She raised the undocumented equipment with carrier facility managers on three separate occasions at three different carrier facilities in two different countries. In each case she was told the equipment was the property of a government agency and was outside the scope of her firm's audit mandate. In each case the carrier's own technical staff demonstrated, through their responses to her questions, that they did not know what the equipment did or who maintained it. It was simply there, installed by someone who was not the carrier, maintained by someone who was not the carrier, connected to something that was not the carrier's network, and entirely outside the audit process that was supposed to account for everything in the facility. She documented the physical characteristics of the equipment, its rack positioning, its cable routing, and the label conventions used on the undocumented cable bundles, in notes she kept outside her firm's document management system. She left the industry in 2021. Her identity and the countries in which she worked have been altered to protect her.*

Britta completed the upgrade on schedule. The parallel bundle is still in the conduit, still routing traffic to wherever it routes traffic, still invisible to every public infrastructure record that covers the municipality. She filed her completion documentation, invoiced the client, and moved to the next job.

She is good at her job. She has built networks across Scandinavia for seventeen years. She understands, at a level that

most people never reach, what infrastructure actually is: it is intention made physical. Every cable, every junction, every splice housing in every conduit exists because someone decided it should exist and paid to put it there. Infrastructure does not appear. It is built. And everything that is built was built for a reason, even the things that do not appear on any public record, especially those things, because the absence from the public record is itself a decision, itself a cost, itself an intention made physical.

The grid that surrounds you was not assembled carelessly. It was assembled with the same precision that goes into any large-scale engineering project, with planning documents and procurement contracts and installation schedules and performance specifications. Those documents exist somewhere. The contracts were signed by someone. The installations were certified by engineers who knew what they were certifying.

You are inside the grid right now. You have been inside it for longer than you know. The question is not how to get outside it. The question is whether you can see it clearly enough to understand what it is doing, because a system you can see is a system you can think about, and thinking about it is the one thing the system was not built to encourage.

Chapter 8

The Cage They Called Security

SCENE

A man named Aleksander is fifty-one years old. He is a civil engineer specializing in transportation infrastructure, based in Warsaw, Poland. He has spent twenty-three years building things: roads, bridges, rail junctions, border crossing facilities. He knows what infrastructure is for because he has read the specifications and the project briefs and the funding applications, and he knows the difference between what a project document says an installation is for and what the installation is actually capable of once it is built.

He is sitting in a site trailer at six in the evening, after the crew has gone, with a set of revised specifications for a border facility upgrade he has been contracted to oversee. The revisions arrived this afternoon from the project's coordinating authority, a European infrastructure funding body he has worked with before. He has been reading them for two hours.

The original specifications called for standard moderniza-

tion: new vehicle lanes, updated customs booths, improved lighting, passenger processing capacity expansion. Standard work. He has done it eight times at six different crossings. He knows what a border crossing modernization looks like.

What is in these revised specifications is not that. The revised specifications include sensor array housings at intervals he has never seen in a civilian crossing design. They include subsurface conduit runs that are not connected to any facility system on the electrical or data schematics he has been given. They include structural reinforcements at the lane barriers rated for vehicle arrest loads that are five times the standard requirement for a crossing of this traffic volume. And they include a separate, locked room in the control building whose purpose is listed in the specifications as administrative storage and whose power and data connections, clearly visible in the building plans, are rated for a server installation roughly equivalent to what a mid-sized data center would require.

Aleksander has been building things for twenty-three years. He knows what administrative storage looks like. He also knows that you do not ask certain questions about certain projects if you want to keep getting certain contracts. He is going to build what the specifications say to build. But he is going to keep a personal copy of the original specs and the revised specs side by side in a folder that he does not keep in the site trailer.

He has been building things his whole career. This is the first time he has felt, with professional certainty, that he was building something he was not being told the full purpose of.

The chokepoint is one of the oldest tools of territorial control in the documented record, the deliberate engineering of geography, natural or artificial, to force movement through a narrow passage where it can be observed, taxed, stopped, or redirected. The Fulda Gap, a lowland corridor in central Germany approximately ninety kilometers wide at its narrowest navigable point, was during the Cold War the primary anticipated invasion route for Warsaw Pact armored forces moving west. It was the most intensively planned, surveyed, and fortified chokepoint in NATO's European defensive architecture.

The answers developed for the Fulda Gap, sensor coverage, layered barriers, observation posts at intervals, communications infrastructure embedded in the physical landscape, became the template for border security infrastructure development across NATO member states in the decades following the Cold War's end. The threat changed. The infrastructure template did not.

Source: Hahn, R.F. (1987). The Fulda Gap and NATO Defense of Western Europe. Military Review. Vol. 67, No. 6. U.S. Army Command and General Staff College, Fort Leavenworth, Kansas.

The European Union's Entry-Exit System creates a centralized database recording the entry and exit of every non-EU national crossing an EU external border. The record includes biometric data: fingerprints and facial images. The system links individual biometric records to movement history across the EU's external border, creating a longitudinal record of every crossing by every registered individual.

The stated purpose is migration and security management. The capability created is a biometric movement database covering every non-EU national crossing any EU external border, linked to individual identity records, updated in real time at every crossing point, and accessible to law enforcement and security agencies across member states. The distance between managing irregular migration and having a comprehensive, real-time biometric tracking system for all cross-border movement is measured in a policy decision, not a technical one. The technical capability, once built, does not care about the policy rationale that funded its construction.

Source: European Commission. Regulation (EU) 2017/2226 of the European Parliament and of the Council establishing an Entry/Exit System. Official Journal of the European Union. L 327, December 9, 2017. Available at eur-lex.europa.eu.

DARPA's Human Terrain System was a real program, not a vault document. It was developed by the U.S. Army and operated in Iraq and Afghanistan between 2007 and 2014 with a total program cost of approximately seven hundred and twenty-six million dollars. Its stated purpose was to provide military commanders with social science analysis of local populations, cultural mapping, tribal structures, and behavioral patterns, to improve the effectiveness of counterinsurgency operations.

What the Human Terrain System demonstrated, at a cost of seven hundred and twenty-six million documented dollars, is that the U.S. military considered the behavioral mapping of civilian populations, their movement patterns, their social networks, their compliance thresholds, a sufficiently important military capability to fund at that scale during active combat operations. The program ended in 2014. The methodology, the application of behavioral and movement data to population management, did not end with it. It migrated into the civilian infrastructure that expanded in exactly the years following the program's closure.

Source: American Anthropological Association. AAA Commission on the Engagement of Anthropology with the US Security and Intelligence Communities. Final Report, October 4, 2007. Available at americananthro.org. See also: Lamb, C.J., et al. (2013). Human Terrain Teams: An Organizational Innovation for Sociocultural Knowledge in Irregular Warfare. Institute of World Politics Press, Washington D.C.

Approximately ninety-five percent of international internet traffic travels through fiber-optic cables laid on the ocean floor. There are currently more than four hundred active undersea cable systems, totalling over one point three million kilometers of cable. Each cable system has a finite number of landing stations, points where the undersea cable comes ashore and connects to terrestrial networks. Those landing stations are the physical chokepoints of the global information infrastructure.

Major landing stations in the United Kingdom, the United States, France, Japan, and Singapore handle disproportionate shares of global traffic because the cable routing geography funnels traffic through them. The NSA's UPSTREAM collection program operated by tapping the fiber-optic cables at or near landing stations, collecting data in transit.

The technical feasibility of that collection was confirmed by the existence of the infrastructure. The landing stations exist. The cables pass through them. The data is physically present at those points. Anyone with access to the landing station has access to the data. Four hundred cable systems. One point three million kilometers. A handful of landing stations where almost all of it comes ashore. Concentration is not an accident of geography. It is a feature of engineering. And features have purposes.

Source: TeleGeography. Submarine Cable Map. PriMetrica, Inc. Available at submarinecablemap.com. See also: Starosielski, N. (2015). The Undersea Network. Duke University Press, Durham, North Carolina.

Composite account, identity protected: *A former senior project manager for a European infrastructure development consortium described the internal process by which specifications for border and transit facility upgrades were developed and communicated to contractors. Standard projects moved through a single specification phase in which the client's requirements were translated into engineering documents and distributed to the contractor for implementation. A category of projects she came to identify by specific funding source characteristics moved through a different process: an initial specification phase that was distributed to the contractor, followed by a secondary specification revision that arrived after contract signing and included system requirements that had not been present in the original document. The secondary specifications consistently included elements that were not connected to the facility's stated operational function: power and data infrastructure rated beyond any civilian operational requirement, structural elements rated for loads that exceeded the facility's traffic projections by significant margins, and separate enclosed spaces whose stated purpose did not account for their power and data connections. Contractors who raised questions about the secondary specifications were told the additional elements were dual-use provisions required by the funding authority's security standards. She managed fourteen projects over eight years that followed this pattern. The funding sources for these projects included bodies whose names appeared in public procurement records and* *bodies whose names did not. She left the consortium in 2020 after a reorganization she described as abrupt and unexplained. Her identity and the countries in which she worked have been altered to protect her current position.*

Aleksander drove home at eight o'clock. He stopped at a junction he has driven through a thousand times and sat at the light for the full cycle without moving, not because he missed the green but because he was thinking about the subsurface conduit runs in the revised specifications, the ones not connected to any facility system he had been given plans for. Conduit runs go somewhere. They are not decorative. Someone specified them, and someone specified where they terminate, and that termination point is in a set of plans that Aleksander was not given.

He drove home. He put the folder with both sets of specifications in the drawer of his desk at home, not the one at the site trailer, and he sat at the kitchen table and thought about the twenty-three years he had spent building things and the number of times he had built something whose full purpose he understood completely versus the number of times he had built something and accepted that the plans he was given were all the plans there were.

He is a precise man. He has built his career on precision, on knowing what the specifications say and what the structure requires and whether those two things match. And what he understands now, sitting at his kitchen table with the specificity that comes from twenty-three years of professional experience, is that the structures he has been building are more capable than the purposes he was told they served.

Every border crossing he has built or upgraded in the last decade can do things that a border crossing does not need to do if its only job is to process legitimate travellers. The sensors are more numerous than that job requires. The structural ratings exceed that job's demands. The data connections feed somewhere that the project documentation does not describe.

He built them anyway because that is what you do when you are a professional with a contract and a crew and a timeline. But he knows what he built. And knowing changes the landscape you move through, because every structure you pass through from this point forward carries the question: what is this actually capable of, and who decided that, and why did they need it to be capable of that here?

The borders were always there. They told you they were for your protection. What they were actually for was management. And management requires infrastructure, and the infrastructure is built, and it is waiting, and it has been waiting long enough that most people have stopped noticing it is there.

CHAPTER 9

It Already Knows You

SCENE

A woman named Priya is thirty-six years old. She is a UX researcher at a technology firm in Bangalore, India. Her job is to study how people interact with digital interfaces: where their eyes go, how long they pause before making a decision, what language in a prompt increases completion rates, what visual arrangement produces the desired action most reliably. She is, in the precise technical language of her profession, an expert in the architecture of choice. She knows how to build an environment in which a person does what you need them to do without experiencing that action as a compulsion. She knows this because she does it every day, for products used by millions of people, and she is good at it.

Tonight she is sitting at her desk at eleven in the evening, not because she has been asked to stay late but because she is reading a paper that a colleague forwarded her three days ago that she has not been able to stop thinking about. The paper is an academic study of behavioral response patterns across a large consumer platform. It is not a classified document. It is published research, peer-reviewed, available through a university library database. It describes, in the standard methodological language of behavioral science, a system for detecting a user's emotional state from interaction patterns, including typing speed, scroll velocity, pause duration before selection, and error rate, and adjusting the interface in real time to produce a target behavioral outcome based on that detected state.

Priya knows this methodology. She uses adjacent versions of it in her own work. What she is looking at right now, at eleven in the evening, is the gap between the version she uses, which she was trained to think of as the boundary of the field, and the version described in this paper, which is significantly beyond that boundary in both sophistication and scope.

She is an expert in the architecture of choice. She knows exactly what this paper is describing. And she knows that if a published paper is describing a system at this level of development, the unpublished operational version of that system is somewhere considerably further along than what she is reading.

She closes the paper. Opens it again. This is the third time she has done this tonight. She is looking for the part where the methodology becomes something other than what she recognizes. She keeps not finding it. The methodology is recognizable all the way through. It is just recognizable at a scale and integration level that she was not aware existed outside of classified research environments.

She is very good at her job. She has just realized that her job

is a small room inside a much larger building whose other rooms she has never been shown.

The behavioral nudge is not a theory of social control. It is a documented academic discipline with a formal research literature, institutional government adoption, and a Nobel Prize awarded to one of its primary architects. Richard Thaler received the 2017 Nobel Memorial Prize in Economic Sciences for his work on behavioral economics, specifically the research demonstrating that human decision-making departs systematically from rational self-interest in predictable, mappable ways, and that the environment in which a choice is presented, the choice architecture, reliably shapes the choice made without the decision-maker's awareness.

The United Kingdom's Behavioral Insights Team was established in 2010 as the first government unit explicitly dedicated to applying behavioral economics to public policy. Its methods involved restructuring the presentation of choices to make the desired outcome the default or the most cognitively accessible option. The unit published its methods and its results. The publication was not reluctant disclosure. It was deliberate demonstration of a capability the government considered valuable enough to formalize, fund, and eventually spin off as a private company with government contracts in multiple countries.

The Behavioral Insights Team's published work documents that modifying the architecture of choice, without changing the choices available, without coercion, without the subject's awareness that the architecture has been designed to produce a specific outcome, reliably changes behavior at population scale. That is the published, peer-reviewed, government-validated conclusion of a decade of applied research.

Source: Thaler, R.H., and Sunstein, C.R. (2008). Nudge: Improving Decisions About Health, Wealth, and Happiness. Yale University Press, New Haven. See also: Behavioral Insights Team. Annual Report 2013-2014. Cabinet Office, London, 2014. Available at bi.team.

DARPA's LifeLog program was proposed in 2003 and canceled in 2004, officially due to privacy concerns. Its stated purpose was to create a continuously updated database of everything a person did, saw, heard, and read, a complete digital record of an individual's life, drawn from sensors, communications devices, and online activity, that could be analyzed to reveal behavioral patterns, preferences, and intentions.

The program was canceled in February 2004. Facebook was founded in February 2004. That correspondence is a matter of public record and has been noted by researchers, journalists, and former intelligence officials without any definitive public explanation of whether it is coincidence or continuity.

What is not coincidence is the functional correspondence between what LifeLog proposed to build and what the major consumer technology platforms proceeded to build in the years following its cancellation. The continuous behavioral record, the pattern analysis, the preference mapping, the intention inference: these are not metaphors for what Facebook, Google, and their successors built. They are operational descriptions. The platforms built LifeLog's architecture using consumer participation and advertising revenue rather than government contracts. The result is functionally identical to what DARPA proposed, scaled to billions of users rather than individual military personnel.

Source: Shachtman, N. (2004). Pentagon Kills LifeLog Project. Wired,

February 4, 2004. Available at wired.com. See also: DARPA. LifeLog Program Solicitation BAA03-30. Defense Advanced Research Projects Agency, Arlington, Virginia, 2003.

The internal research conducted by major platforms on their ability to influence user emotional states and behavioral outcomes is partially visible through regulatory proceedings, academic publications, and disclosed internal documents. The U.S. Senate Commerce Committee conducted hearings in 2021 on the internal research practices of major social media platforms following the disclosure of internal documents showing that platform researchers had documented the negative psychological effects of their products on specific user populations and had not acted on those findings.

The disclosed documents showed that the major consumer technology platforms possess, and have possessed for years, a detailed, empirically validated understanding of how their design choices affect user psychology and behavior, and that this understanding is applied deliberately to product development. The platforms know exactly what their design choices do to user psychology. The knowledge is documented in their own internal research. The knowledge informs product decisions. The product decisions shape the behavioral environment of billions of people every day.

Source: U.S. Senate Committee on Commerce, Science, and Transportation. Hearings on Protecting Kids Online. 117th Congress, 2021-2022. Available at commerce.senate.gov. See also: Glazer, E., et al. The Facebook Files. The Wall Street Journal. September-October 2021.

Project Iceworm was a real United States Army program, conducted between 1960 and 1966 beneath the Greenland ice sheet. The program successfully constructed a network of tunnels at Camp Century, a facility built under the ice using nuclear power, that housed laboratory facilities, living quarters, and operational infrastructure for military personnel. The tunnels were constructed using cut-and-cover technique, in which trenches were cut into the ice surface, prefabricated structures were placed in the trenches, and the ice was allowed to close over them. The resulting tunnels were stable, insulated, and invisible from the surface.

What Project Iceworm demonstrated, at full operational scale and with documented success, is that a functional, sustained human installation can be constructed and operated beneath polar ice, using nuclear power, invisible from the surface, for an extended operational period. The United States Army did this in 1960. With 1960 technology. The question of what a program with the same objective, executed with six decades of subsequent technological development, would be capable of producing is not a metaphysical question. It is an engineering question. And the documented baseline for that question is Camp Century.

Source: U.S. Army Cold Regions Research and Engineering Laboratory. Camp Century: City Under the Ice. CRREL Technical Report, Hanover, New Hampshire, 1965.

Composite account, identity protected: *A former data scientist who spent seven years working on behavioral prediction systems for a major technology platform described the internal capability his team had developed for inferring user emotional state from interaction data in real time. The system did not require access to camera or microphone data to produce accurate emotional state assessments. It used typing cadence, scroll behavior, tap pressure on touchscreens, and the time* *pattern of application switching to generate a continuous emotional state score for each active user. The score was accurate enough, validated against ground truth data collected through other means in controlled research settings, that it was used operationally to determine the timing and content of notifications, the ranking of content in personalized feeds, and the sequencing of prompts designed to drive specific user actions. The emotional state scores were not stored as named user attributes in the systems he had access to, but were computed in real time and consumed by the ranking and notification systems before being discarded, which meant they did not appear in user data export files and were not visible to users exercising data access rights under privacy regulations. He said his team understood this architectural choice as a deliberate decision to keep the emotional state inference capability outside the scope of regulatory data access requirements. He left the platform in 2022 after a reorganization that dissolved his team and folded its work into a larger personalization infrastructure group whose internal documentation he was not given access to. His identity and the name of the platform have been altered to protect him.*

Priya closed her laptop at midnight. She sat in the dark of her office for a few minutes before she got up. She is going to go home. She is going to sleep. She is going to come back tomorrow and do her job, which is to design choice architectures that produce target behavioral outcomes for products used by millions of people.

She is going to do all of that with the specific knowledge, acquired tonight, that the version of the field she works in is the visible room. The building it sits inside is larger than she was shown, and the rooms she was not shown are doing what her

room does, at scales and with capabilities that the published research literature represents as an edge case rather than a baseline.

She has spent her career making systems that know what people will do before the people know they are going to do it. She is very good at this. She designed it with care and professionalism and the understanding that she was operating at the edge of what was possible.

She was not at the edge. She was in the foyer. The building goes back much further than the foyer. And what it contains, running continuously, on devices that are in every pocket and on every street and in every home, is a system that has been learning the population it runs on since before most of the population understood that something was learning them.

You are not surveilled in the crude sense of being watched. You are modeled. There is a representation of you, built from years of interaction data, that predicts your responses before you have them, that knows which presentation of a choice will produce the desired outcome before you have seen the choice, that has been refined by your own behavior into something more accurate than your own self-assessment. That model is not in your phone. It is in infrastructure you do not own and cannot access and were never told existed.

The system does not need to force you. It learned you well enough that it does not have to. Forcing people is expensive and visible and generates resistance. Knowing them well enough to arrange the environment so that they choose correctly on their own, that is the architecture. That is what was

built. And it has been running long enough that the version of yourself you experience as free and self-determining has been shaped by it for longer than you have known it existed.

That is not surveillance. That is something more fundamental than surveillance. It is the reengineering of the conditions under which you become yourself. And it is already done.

CHAPTER 10

They Didn't Count It All

SCENE

A man named Okonkwo is forty-seven years old. He is an amateur astronomer and secondary school science teacher in Enugu, Nigeria.

He has been watching the sky for twenty-one years with progressively better equipment, beginning with a borrowed refractor telescope and arriving, after two decades of patient saving, at a twelve-inch Dobsonian reflector that he built himself from a kit and set up in the courtyard behind his house. He knows the sky above Enugu the way a cartographer knows a map: every regular feature, every seasonal shift, every object that belongs and every object that does not.

He does not work for any government or any institution.

He is a science teacher who watches the sky because the sky interests him, and because the sky above Enugu at two in the morning, away from the city's main light sources, is genuinely

beautiful, and because he is the kind of man who believes that looking carefully at things is one of the few activities that consistently returns more than it costs.

Tonight he has been watching for three hours. At 2:47 in the morning he observes a pass by an object that he cannot match to any entry in the catalogs he uses: Heavens-Above, Celestrak, the JPL Horizons database. The object is not faint. It is a magnitude-two pass, well within naked-eye visibility, following a polar orbit at an estimated altitude consistent with low Earth orbit. It transits his field in approximately ninety seconds. It shows no tumbling, no flashing, no solar panel glint. It is steady, dark, and moving with the deliberate regularity of something under active attitude control.

He checks his catalogs again. He cross-references the transit time and azimuth against every object in the Space-Track TLE database that would have been above his horizon at that time. Nothing matches. He notes the observation in his log, as he notes everything, with time, azimuth, elevation arc, estimated magnitude, and a brief description. In the description field he writes: unidentified, uncatalogued, polar orbit, no optical signature consistent with passive object.

He has made this notation before. Not often. But before.

He is not alarmed. He is a patient man who believes in looking carefully and noting what he sees. What he sees tonight is an object in the sky that is not in any list of objects that are supposed to be in the sky. He does not know what that means. He knows that it means something.

The number of objects in Earth orbit is not a settled figure. It is a contested one, and the contest is not between scientists with different measurement methodologies. It is between the public record and the operational record, two datasets that have diverged significantly and whose divergence is documented, acknowledged, and unexplained by the institutions responsible for both.

The U.S. Space Surveillance Network, operated by the United States Space Force, tracks objects in Earth orbit using a global network of radar and optical sensors. The network's public catalog lists approximately twenty-seven thousand objects as of recent counts. Of those, approximately five thousand are active satellites. The remainder are debris: defunct satellites, rocket bodies, and fragmentation objects.

The classified catalog is larger. The existence of a classified layer of the orbital catalog is not disputed. The United States government officially acknowledges that it tracks objects that are not listed in the public catalog, on the grounds that publishing their orbital parameters would reveal classified capabilities. Multiple independent analysts have concluded that the classified layer contains a minimum of several hundred objects whose orbital parameters are withheld from the public record. They are up there. The government knows they are up there. You are not told they are up there.

Source: Union of Concerned Scientists. UCS Satellite Database. Updated periodically. Available at ucsusa.org/resources/satellite-database. See also: Weeden, B. (2010). Overview of the Legal and Policy Frameworks for Space Situational Awareness Data Sharing. Secure World Foundation Technical Report. Available at swfound.org.

The Sura Ionospheric Heating Facility is a real installation operated by the Russian Institute of Radiophysics and Electronics near Vasilsursk in the Nizhny Novgorod region. It consists of an array of high-power radio transmitters capable of directing intense radio frequency energy into the ionosphere. The facility has been operational since 1981.

Sura is the Russian counterpart to HAARP, addressed in Chapter 7. Like HAARP, its capability profile extends to applications not fully described in the public scientific literature. The generation of ELF waves through ionospheric heating is not a classified finding. It is published in peer-reviewed research from both Sura and HAARP.

Heating the ionosphere at audio frequencies modulates the ionospheric conductivity, which in turn modulates naturally occurring ionospheric currents, producing ELF radiation that propagates through the Earth-ionosphere waveguide. The ELF waves produced by this mechanism can propagate globally. They are in the frequency range that overlaps with human neurological bands. Both facilities are capable of producing them. Both facilities have done so in documented experiments.

Source: Golkowski, M., et al. (2008). Multistation observations of ELF/VLF whistlers and triggered emissions excited by the HAARP facility. Journal of Geophysical Research: Space Physics. Vol. 113, No. A10. American Geophysical Union. doi:10.1029/2008JA013305.

The Senate Select Committee on Intelligence hearings on MKULTRA, conducted in 1977, were triggered by the discovery of MKULTRA documents that had survived the 1973 destruction order issued by CIA Director Richard Helms. The surviving documents provided, for the first time, specific details of MKULTRA subprojects that had not been disclosed in the earlier Church Committee review.

Among the subprojects documented in the 1977 hearing record was research into the behavioral effects of electromagnetic frequency exposure on human subjects. The research investigated the possibility of inducing specific psychological states, including disorientation, compliance, and altered sleep patterns, through controlled electromagnetic field exposure. The documented objective of that research is important to read precisely: not understanding the effects of electromagnetic exposure for health or safety purposes, but developing techniques for behavioral control. That is what was funded. That is what was researched. The specific findings are in the portions of the MKULTRA record that were destroyed in 1973. What survived is sufficient to document the program's objectives and methods. The findings themselves were apparently considered important enough to destroy. The research did not stop in 1977. The hearings stopped. The research had already moved.

Source: U.S. Senate Select Committee on Intelligence. Project MKULTRA, The CIA's Program of Research in Behavioral Modification. Joint Hearing, 95th Congress, 1st Session, August 3, 1977. U.S. Government Printing Office, Washington D.C.

The Schumann Resonance is a set of electromagnetic resonance frequencies that exist in the cavity between the Earth's surface and the ionosphere. The fundamental Schumann Resonance frequency is approximately 7.83 Hz, with harmonics at approximately 14.3, 20.8, 27.3, and 33.8 Hz. These frequencies overlap with human brainwave frequencies in the alpha and theta bands. The research into the relationship between the Earth's electromagnetic environment and human neurological function is not fringe science. It is published in peer-reviewed journals and has been pursued by researchers at institutions including the National Institutes of Health.

What the monitoring record shows, over the decades of continuous measurement, is that Schumann Resonance frequencies are not perfectly stable. Among the anomalies in the monitoring record are episodes of significant amplitude and frequency deviation that do not correspond to known natural drivers. These anomalies appear in the monitoring data. They are noted in published research. They are not explained by the natural variability models that account for routine fluctuations in the record. A global electromagnetic resonance in the frequency range of human brainwave activity. Anomalies not explained by natural variability. A documented research program into electromagnetic behavioral modification being actively developed by intelligence agencies in the same frequency range. These are three separate documented facts. What connects them is not speculation.

Source: Schumann, W.O. (1952). Uber die strahlungslosen Eigenschwingungen einer leitenden Kugel. Zeitschrift fur Naturforschung A. Vol. 7, pp. 149-154. See also: Cherry, N. (2002). Schumann Resonances, a plausible biophysical mechanism for the human health effects of Solar/Geomagnetic Activity. Natural Hazards. Vol. 26, pp. 279-331. Springer.

Composite account, identity protected: *A former satellite systems engineer who spent fourteen years working on classified government satellite programs in a NATO member country described the internal classification structure applied to orbital assets within the programs he worked on. The programs maintained two distinct asset registers: a* *primary register that was shared with program oversight authorities and contained the assets that appeared in the classified national intelligence satellite catalog, and a secondary register that was maintained within the program itself and not shared with oversight authorities, containing assets whose existence was known only to the program's senior technical staff and their operational counterparts in the intelligence community. The secondary register assets were not rogue or unauthorized in any sense he understood: they had program numbers, maintenance schedules, and operational tasking orders like any other asset. They simply did not appear in the oversight register. He said he understood this arrangement to be standard practice across multiple programs he was aware of, not an anomaly specific to the programs he worked on directly. The orbital parameters of secondary register assets were maintained by the same tracking infrastructure that maintained the primary register, but the data was tagged to prevent it from populating the shared catalog feeds. He described this as a routing decision, not a concealment decision, though he acknowledged that the practical effect was identical. He left the industry in 2018 following a medical event that he attributes in part to working conditions during an extended operational period. His identity and nationality have been altered to protect him.*

Okonkwo logged the unidentified object and went inside at four in the morning. He made tea. He sat at the kitchen table and thought about what he had seen with the specific quality of attention he brings to things that do not fit: patient, precise, reluctant to conclude more than the evidence supports and equally reluctant to conclude less.

He has spent twenty-one years watching the sky above Enugu. He has logged thousands of passes by objects whose

identity he can verify against the public catalogs. He has logged, in those twenty-one years, eleven passes by objects he could not match to any cataloged entry. Eleven unidentified, uncatalogued objects in polar or near-polar orbits, observed from the same location over two decades, logged with the same methodology, cross-referenced against every public database available to him.

Eleven is not a large number. It is not a number that proves anything by itself. But it is a number that has a meaning, which is that in twenty-one years of careful sky watching, a dedicated amateur astronomer in Nigeria, using publicly available databases and consumer-grade equipment, has observed eleven objects that the public record says should not be there.

Multiply that by the number of people watching the sky around the world. Multiply it by the fraction of those observations that get cross-referenced and logged rather than dismissed.

Multiply it by the decades of monitoring data sitting in amateur astronomy notebooks and observation logs that no one has assembled into a systematic analysis.

The objects are there. Okonkwo saw one tonight. He has seen ten before tonight. They are in orbits that suggest purpose and maintenance. They show no passive object signatures. They follow paths that the public catalog does not account for.

He does not know what they are. He knows that they exist and that the record that is supposed to account for every-

thing in the sky above him does not account for them. That is all he knows with certainty.

It is, as it happens, quite a lot. Because a record that does not account for what exists is not a complete record. And a system that operates in the gap between the complete record and the public record is a system that made a decision about what you were allowed to know about the sky above your own head.

That decision was made without your input. The objects are still up there. They were there last night. They will be there tomorrow night. And the catalog that is supposed to tell you what is above you will continue, tomorrow night and the night after, to say nothing about them at all.

CHAPTER 11

What Byrd Found

SCENE

A woman named Leonora is forty-nine years old. She is a naval historian based in Lisbon, Portugal, specializing in the history of polar exploration and the documentation of classified military expeditions. She has spent twenty-two years in the intersection of official military history and the gaps in that history: the expeditions whose records are complete, the expeditions whose records contain lacunae that the official finding aids describe as accidental, and the specific category of expedition whose records were complete until they were reclassified, at which point the finding aids began describing the reclassified sections as unavailable pending review.

She has learned, over twenty-two years, to read the shape of a classified section the way a radiologist reads the shape of an absence on an imaging scan. The absence has a form. The form tells you something about what is missing even when the content is not accessible.

She is sitting in her study on a Thursday evening with three

documents spread across her desk. The first is a publicly available copy of the official after-action report for Operation Highjump. The second is a transcript of a press interview given by Rear Admiral Richard E. Byrd in March 1947, shortly after his return from the expedition. The third is a list of the specific sections of the Operation Highjump documentation that were reclassified between 1954 and 1958 and whose current classification status she has been unable to determine through Freedom of Information Act requests submitted over the past seven years.

She is not looking at these documents for the first time. She has been examining the Operation Highjump record for nine years. What she is doing tonight is the thing she does periodically when she has gathered enough new information from adjacent archival research to return to the core documents with fresh attention: she is reading the shape of the absence.

The official after-action report describes a successful scientific expedition that accomplished its stated mapping and reconnaissance objectives. The press interview describes something different. The reclassified sections describe something that neither the official report nor the press interview fully accounts for. The relationship between those three silences is the question Leonora has been working on for nine years.

She picks up the press interview transcript and begins reading it again from the beginning.

Operation Highjump was the largest military expedition ever mounted to Antarctica. Its scale was not consistent with a scientific mapping program: 4,700 military personnel, 13 ships including an aircraft carrier and a submarine, 23 aircraft, and a budget whose classified components have never been fully disclosed. It was commanded by Rear Admiral Richard E. Byrd, the most experienced polar explorer in American history.

The expedition was abruptly terminated weeks ahead of its planned schedule in February 1947. The official explanation for the early termination was deteriorating weather conditions. The expedition had been planned to last six to eight months. It lasted approximately two months of active field operations before withdrawal was ordered.

Byrd's subsequent public statements did not reflect the official account of a successful scientific program terminated by weather. In a press conference in Chile on March 5, 1947, Byrd stated that the United States needed to be prepared for the possibility of attack from aircraft capable of flying from pole to pole at incredible speeds. It was not a statement consistent with the conclusion of a scientific mapping expedition whose primary challenge had been adverse weather. In subsequent years Byrd described Antarctica as a strategic area of vital importance and, in a 1954 interview, described the possibility of lands beyond the pole whose existence he considered significant to the security of the United States. The specific phrase lands beyond the pole appears in multiple documented accounts of Byrd's statements in the years following Operation Highjump.

Source: Rose, L. (2008). Explorer: The Life of Richard E. Byrd. University of Missouri Press, Columbia. See also: Bertrand, K.J. (1971). Americans in Antarctica 1775-1948. American Geographical Society, New York.

The Bedford Level experiment constitutes one of the most extensively documented empirical investigations of the Earth's surface geometry in the scientific record. Samuel Birley Rowbotham conducted the original experiment in 1838 on the Old Bedford River in Cambridgeshire, England, a remarkably straight six-mile canal whose surface provided an ideal test bed for observing whether the expected curvature of the Earth would produce the predicted drop in the visibility of objects observed across the water's surface. Rowbotham observed objects across the six-mile stretch and found that objects remained visible at distances at which the curvature model predicted they would have dropped below the horizon by several feet.

Alfred Russel Wallace, the co-discoverer with Charles Darwin of the theory of natural selection, conducted a formally structured repetition of the Bedford Level experiment in 1870. Wallace's repetition used three poles of equal height positioned at measured intervals along the canal and observed through a telescope to determine whether the middle pole appeared above or below the line connecting the two outer poles. Wallace observed the middle pole appearing above the line connecting the outer poles and interpreted this as consistent with the curvature model. The dispute between Wallace and his challenger became one of the most extensively documented scientific controversies of the Victorian era, producing years of correspondence, legal proceedings, and public argument documented in the scientific and popular press of the period. The controversy was never resolved in the clean, definitive manner that the standard presentation of the globe model implies it was.

Source: Garwood, C. (2007). Flat Earth: The History of an Infamous Idea. Macmillan, London. See also: Wallace, A.R. (1905). My Life: A

Record of Events and Opinions. Chapman and Hall, London. Vol. 2.

NASA has publicly acknowledged that its iconic Blue Marble photographs of the Earth are composite images assembled from multiple satellite data sources rather than single photographic exposures. The 2002 Blue Marble image is described in NASA's own documentation as a composite assembled from data collected over a period of months and processed using software that combined multiple passes to produce a cloud-free representation of the Earth's surface. It is not a photograph in the conventional sense of a single exposure capturing a moment in time. It is a constructed representation produced by combining and processing data from multiple sources.

The documented existence of editorial decisions in the construction of NASA's official Earth imagery is the relevant fact for the dome framework. The construction process provides the opportunity. Whether that opportunity has been used to produce imagery that systematically excludes or modifies specific atmospheric or surface features consistent with the dome's existence is a question the public record does not answer because the specific technical parameters of the editorial decisions are not publicly disclosed.

Source: NASA Goddard Space Flight Center. (2002). Blue Marble: Land Surface, Ocean Color, Sea Ice and Clouds. NASA Earth Observatory. Available at earthobservatory.nasa.gov.

The pattern that cross-cultural comparison of indigenous traditions reveals is not the content of any individual tradition but the structural consistency across traditions whose carriers have no documented historical contact. Cultures separated by oceans and millennia independently maintain traditions about inhabited territories beyond the known world. The Hopi tradition of emergence describes the current world as the fourth world, entered through an opening after the destruction of the previous three. The Norse cosmological tradition describes nine worlds of which the human world is only one. The Inuit traditions of multiple Arctic cultures describe a land beyond the northern ice where the sun shines continuously and beings of great capability dwell.

The academic literature treats the structural consistency of cross-cultural mythological traditions as evidence for universal features of human psychology. The vault framework treats the same structural consistency as evidence for a common historical source: fragmentary memories transmitted through the oral record of reset-cycle survivors, degraded by centuries of retelling without the context that would have made them geographically specific, but structurally consistent across widely separated cultures because they share a common origin in genuine geographical knowledge.

Source: Leeming, D.A. (2010). Creation Myths of the World: An Encyclopedia. 2nd edition. ABC-CLIO, Santa Barbara, California. See also: Eliade, M. (1964). Shamanism: Archaic Techniques of Ecstasy. Princeton University Press, Princeton, New Jersey.

Composite account, identity protected: *A former military intelligence analyst who spent sixteen years working on polar region assessments described the specific documents from the Operation Highjump classified archive that she had access to in the course of her work and what those documents contained that was not in the public record. The classified portions of the Operation Highjump record included after-action reports from specific aircraft crews describing visual ob-*

servations made during flights over the interior of the continent that were not consistent with the terrain features shown on the expedition's official maps of those areas. The observations described by multiple independent crews in separate reports included structured formations in areas that the official maps showed as featureless ice, and aerial observations of openings in the ice surface at specific coordinates that the official maps did not indicate. The documents she accessed also included a medical section covering treatment of personnel for conditions whose described symptoms were consistent with exposure to directed electromagnetic radiation, conditions for which the standard after-action report listed only cold injury and frostbite. Those medical sections were classified at a higher level than the rest of the expedition record. She had no way of verifying what the crews had actually observed or what had produced the medical conditions, only that the classified record described both in terms that were not consistent with a routine scientific mapping expedition terminated by weather. Her identity and the agency she worked for have been altered to protect her.

Leonora finishes reading the press interview transcript at ten o'clock in the evening. She has read it many times before. She reads it again tonight because she has spent nine years learning to read the shape of the absence and because the shape of what is missing in the public record of Operation Highjump has been clarified by a document she obtained last month through an archival contact in Washington.

The document is a memo from the Office of Naval Intelligence dated June 1947, four months after Operation Highjump's early termination. It is not classified. It was declassified in the 1980s as part of a routine review. It was cataloged in a finding

aid. It has not been published or analyzed in any scholarly work she has been able to locate. The memo refers, without elaboration, to the preparation of separate operational files for the Highjump materials designated as requiring extended review before disposition, and it lists the specific officers responsible for managing those files.

The phrase extended review before disposition is the phrase that Naval Intelligence used in 1947 for materials that were being reclassified above their original classification level. The files designated for extended review included three sections whose subject headings in the original finding aid described aerial reconnaissance results from interior Antarctic sectors and anomalous terrain observations requiring follow-up survey.

The official after-action report contains no anomalous terrain observations. The aerial reconnaissance results from interior Antarctic sectors in the public record are unremarkable. The sections designated for extended review describe something that was in the record in June 1947 and was removed from the accessible record before the finding aids were finalized.

What Byrd found beyond the pole is in those sections. What those sections contain has been in extended review since 1947. Leonora has been submitting Freedom of Information Act requests for seven years.

The response to each request has been the same: the records you have described cannot be located in the holdings of the agency you have addressed, and we suggest you contact the following offices.

She contacts the following offices. They cannot locate the records either.

The shape of the absence is the answer she has. What the absence contains is the answer the classification system was built to prevent her from having. The wall is real. What is beyond it was found.

The expedition that found it was the largest military operation ever conducted in the region. The expedition was terminated early. The records of what it found were reclassified. The admiral who led it described the need to prepare for attack from craft flying pole to pole at incredible speeds.

What Byrd found is in the classified record. The classified record is maintained by people who understand what it contains and have determined that you should not. Leonora has spent nine years working toward it. She will spend nine more if that is what it takes.

The absence has a shape. The shape is the evidence. The evidence is enough.

CHAPTER 12

Written Before You Were Born

SCENE

A woman named Fatima is fifty-three years old. She is a financial journalist in Tunis, Tunisia. She has covered North African and Mediterranean economic affairs for twenty-six years. She has interviewed finance ministers, central bank governors, IMF delegation heads, and treasury officials across eleven countries. She has watched economies stabilize and collapse. She has read the explanations offered for both and she has learned, over twenty-six years of professional practice, to distinguish between an explanation that accounts for what happened and an explanation that is offered because something must be said.

She is sitting in her home office at seven in the morning with four browser tabs open, each showing a different country's central bank announcement from the previous forty-eight hours. The announcements are from the European Central Bank, the Bank of England, the Reserve Bank of Australia, and the South African Reserve Bank. Four separate institutions, four separate economies, four separate stated rationales. The announcements are not identical. But the decisions are. All four institutions, within a thirty-six hour window, moved their benchmark interest rates by the same increment in the same direction and used language in their public communications that, while not word-for-word the same, describes the same threat assessment, the same weighting of inflation against growth risk, the same forward guidance horizon.

Fatima has been covering central bank policy for twenty-six years. She knows that central banks communicate with each other. She knows that the Bank for International Settlements in Basel serves as a coordinating forum for global monetary policy. She knows that policy convergence happens. She has written about it many times.

What she has not written about, because she has never been able to source it cleanly enough to publish, is the specific question that is sitting in front of her this morning: at what point does coordination become something more than coordination? At what point does the simultaneity of independent institutional decisions, across different economies with different conditions, become a pattern that coordination alone does not explain?

She has been asking this question privately for eleven years. She has never found the sentence that would let her put it in print. She is looking at four central bank announcements and she is asking it again, and the answer she keeps arriving at is the same answer she has been arriving at for eleven years, which is that the coordination infrastructure for global mon-

etary policy is more integrated, more centralized, and more directive than any of the institutions involved will formally acknowledge.

She knows what coordination looks like. She has covered it for twenty-six years. This looks like something with a single author.

The Bank for International Settlements was established in 1930 under the Hague Agreements. Its stated founding purpose became obsolete almost immediately: the reparations system it was created to administer collapsed within two years. The institution did not collapse with it. It reorganized around a new function that has defined it ever since: serving as a bank for central banks, a settlement institution for international financial transactions between national monetary authorities, and a coordinating forum for global monetary policy.

The BIS is not a national institution. It is not subject to the regulatory authority of any single government. Its assets are immune from seizure, its communications are immune from interception under its own charter, and its senior staff hold diplomatic immunity in Switzerland, where it is headquartered. These immunities are foundational provisions negotiated specifically to place the institution outside the reach of any national legal or regulatory framework.

The BIS hosts the meetings of the Global Economy Meeting, a body comprising the governors of the world's major central banks that meets in Basel every two months. The meetings are not public. The agenda is not published. The conclusions are not disclosed in formal minutes available to the public. What emerges from the meetings is visible only through the subsequent behavior of the central banks whose governors attended. A supranational institution with diplomatic immunity, no public minutes of its senior coordination meetings, and a membership comprising the governors of every major central bank in the world. This is not conspiracy theory. This is the governance architecture of global monetary policy, documented in the institution's own annual reports.

Source: Lebor, A. (2013). Tower of Basel: The Shadowy History of the Secret Bank that Runs the World. PublicAffairs, New York. See also: Bank for International Settlements. 85th Annual Report. Basel, June 2015. Available at bis.org.

The Robertson Panel convened in January 1952 under the direction of the CIA's Office of Scientific Intelligence. Its conclusions are routinely summarized as a determination that UFO reports posed no direct threat to national security. That summary is technically accurate and substantively incomplete. The panel's actual recommendations called for a public debunking campaign to reduce public interest in UFO reports, for the surveillance of civilian UFO research organizations on the grounds that their communications channels could be used by hostile intelligence services, and for the use of mass media to associate UFO reports with the credulous and the uninformed.

Those are not the recommendations of a panel that found nothing worth worrying about. Those are the recommendations of a panel that found something it decided the public should not think seriously about, and that proceeded to design a communications strategy to prevent them from doing so. The strategy is in the declassified report. The report is in the public record. The recommendation was implemented. The implementation is visible in six decades of official dismissal of a subject that the panel's own deliberations treated with sufficient seriousness to require active management of public perception.

Source: Robertson, H.P., et al. Report of the Scientific Advisory Panel on Unidentified Flying Objects. CIA Office of Scientific Intelligence, January 17, 1953. Declassified 1966. Available through National Security Archive, George Washington University, nsarchive.gwu.edu.

Operation Gladio is not a theory. It is a documented program, confirmed by official government acknowledgment in multiple countries, investigated by parliamentary inquiries in Italy, Belgium, and Switzerland, and described in declassified CIA and NATO documents. Its existence was publicly confirmed in 1990 when Italian Prime Minister Giulio Andreotti disclosed to the Italian parliament that a clandestine armed network had operated in Italy since the end of World War II, under NATO oversight, funded and equipped by the CIA, without the knowledge of the Italian parliament or the Italian public.

The Italian parliamentary investigation documented specific operations including involvement in domestic political violence, false flag terrorist attacks, and the manipulation of political outcomes in member countries to prevent electoral results that the network's supervisors considered strategically unacceptable. These are the findings of national parliamentary bodies with subpoena authority, documented in the formal records of those bodies. What Gladio demonstrates is that a parallel governance structure operated beneath the visible political institutions of Western European democracies for decades, directing political outcomes through methods those democracies' citizens had not authorized and were not informed of, under the authority of an external coordinating body not accountable to any of the national parliaments whose political processes it was managing.

Source: Ganser, D. (2005). NATO's Secret Armies: Operation GLADIO and Terrorism in Western Europe. Frank Cass, London. See also: Italian Senate. Parliamentary Commission on Terrorism in Italy and the Causes of the Failure to Identify the Perpetrators Responsible for the Massacre. Final Report, 2000. Rome.

Project Pandora was a classified research program conducted jointly by the U.S. Navy and the CIA beginning in the 1960s, initiated in response to the discovery that the Soviet Union had been directing microwave radiation at the U.S. Embassy in Moscow for decades. Project Pandora investigated the biological and behavioral effects of low-level microwave and radiofrequency radiation on human subjects, examining effects on neurological function, cognitive performance, emotional regulation, and behavioral patterns. It was conducted under conditions that did not meet the standards of informed consent required for human subjects research. Its findings were classified.

The Moscow Signal itself was acknowledged by the U.S. State Department in 1976, after years of denial. The research confirmed measurable behavioral and neurological effects from low-level RF exposure at field strengths achievable by the transmission infrastructure documented across this book's preceding chapters. The connection between the research and the infrastructure is the question the classified record was designed to prevent you from asking.

Source: Steneck, N.H. (1984). The Microwave Debate. MIT Press, Cambridge, Massachusetts. See also: U.S. House of Representatives, Com-

mittee on Commerce. The Soviet Microwave Transmission at the American Embassy: Biological Effects. Hearings, 95th Congress, 1977. U.S. Government Printing Office, Washington D.C.

Composite account, identity protected: *A former senior economist who spent sixteen years working for an international financial institution described the internal coordination mechanisms that operated below the level of formal governance structures. The publicly visible coordination forums were not where the substantive coordination decisions were made. The substantive coordination happened in smaller, less formal settings whose participants were drawn from the senior staff of central banks, finance ministries, and international institutions, not the principals themselves but their most senior technical advisors, people whose names did not appear in press releases and whose participation in coordination meetings was not publicly disclosed. These informal coordination mechanisms produced working agreements that were then implemented through the formal institutional processes of the participating organizations, creating a documentary record that showed independent institutional decisions producing convergent outcomes, rather than a record of the coordination process that produced them. The informal coordination extended beyond monetary policy to regulatory frameworks, to capital flow management, and to crisis response sequencing in ways that produced policy outcomes that appeared synchronized across independent national institutions because they were synchronized, through a coordination process that the formal governance record did not reflect. He left the institution in 2017. His identity and the name of the institution have been altered to protect him.*

Fatima published a piece that afternoon about the central bank announcements. She wrote what she could source:

the coordination forums, the BIS meetings, the documented mechanisms of international monetary policy alignment. She wrote it carefully and accurately and it said less than what she knows.

She has been doing this for twenty-six years. She knows the difference between what she can source and what she knows. She knows that the sourced version, the documented version, the version that passes editorial review and legal review and the professional standards of international financial journalism, is accurate and incomplete. She knows that the incomplete part is not a gap in the evidence. It is a gap in the public record, and the gap in the public record is itself the evidence, because records do not have gaps by accident. Records have gaps because someone made a decision about what would and would not be in them.

The coordination she has been covering for twenty-six years produces decisions that look like independent institutional judgments. They are not. The institutions that produce them are coordinating through mechanisms whose existence is documented at the general level and whose specific operations are not in any public record she has been given access to. The BIS meets. The minutes are not published. The central banks announce. The announcements converge. The gap between those two facts is where the governance actually happens.

She is a journalist. She believes in the sentence that can be sourced. She believes in the documented fact and the named institution and the verifiable record. She has spent twenty-six years inside those standards and she respects them. But she

also knows that a system sophisticated enough to produce coordinated global outcomes through mechanisms that do not appear in the public record is a system that was specifically designed to be invisible to the standards she works within.

You are governed by a system you did not consent to and were not told about. That is not a claim that requires a vault document to support. It is the documented architecture of the institutions that govern you, read carefully, with attention to what the gaps contain.

Chapter 13

They Buried It On Purpose

SCENE

A man named Dmitri is sixty-one years old. He is a structural geologist based in Tbilisi, Georgia, recently retired from a thirty-four year career conducting subsurface surveys for mining and infrastructure development across the Caucasus region and Central Asia. He has spent his professional life reading what is under the ground. He knows how to interpret seismic data, how to identify the difference between natural formation and engineered void, how to look at a subsurface scan and understand what produced the geometry he is seeing.

He is sitting on the terrace of his apartment on a Tuesday afternoon in October, a cup of tea going cold beside him, looking at a printout of a seismic survey result that a former colleague sent him two weeks ago with a note that said simply: tell me what you see.

The survey is from a region in Central Asia he knows well from

his working years. He has run surveys in this area before. He knows the subsurface geology. He knows what the natural formation profile looks like at depth. What he is looking at in this printout does not match the natural formation profile. At a depth of approximately four hundred meters, the seismic return shows a series of voids with geometry that his thirty-four years of professional experience tells him unambiguously did not form naturally. The angles are too precise. The linear extent is too consistent. The depth signature is uniform in a way that natural cavities, formed by dissolution, tectonic stress, or hydrological action, are not.

He has looked at this printout every day for two weeks. He has tried four different interpretive frameworks. Each one reaches the same conclusion. There is something down there that was made, not formed. It is at a depth that precludes recent construction by any conventional method he is aware of. And it is in a location where, according to every geological map and every institutional record he has access to, there is nothing.

He is sixty-one years old and recently retired and he has spent thirty-four years reading what is under the ground. He knows what he is looking at. What he does not know is what to do with it, because the institutional channels through which a finding like this would normally be reported are the same institutional channels that produced the geological maps that say nothing is there.

He picks up his tea. It is cold. He sets it back down. He looks at the printout. The geometry is still there. It does not change because he has looked at it for two weeks. It does not become

natural formation because he would prefer a simpler answer. It is what it is, and what it is has no place in any record he has been given.

Göbekli Tepe is a site in southeastern Turkey whose excavation, beginning in 1994, produced findings that fundamentally disrupted the established timeline of organized human civilization. The site consists of carved stone pillars arranged in circular enclosures, the largest of which weigh up to twenty tons and are carved with detailed relief images of animals and abstract symbols. Radiocarbon dating places the site's construction at approximately 11,600 years before the present, making it approximately seven thousand years older than Stonehenge and predating the development of agriculture, cities, and writing by several thousand years in the established archaeological chronology.

Ground-penetrating radar surveys of the site, conducted by a team from the German Archaeological Institute and published in 2019, revealed that the structures currently excavated represent approximately five percent of the site's total extent. The remaining ninety-five percent is unexcavated. The radar surveys show additional enclosures, additional pillar arrays, and at greater depth, anomalies in the subsurface profile that the published survey describes as requiring further investigation. The nature of those deeper anomalies has not been the subject of published follow-up research. Access to the site for independent researchers requires permits issued by the Turkish Ministry of Culture, and the conditions of those permits determine what can be studied and what cannot. Ninety-five percent unexcavated. Subsurface anomalies at depth requiring further investigation. Further investigation not published. Access controlled by government permit.

Source: Schmidt, K. (2010). Göbekli Tepe: The Stone Age Sanctuaries. Documenta Praehistorica. Vol. 37, pp. 239-256. University of Ljubljana. See also: Dietrich, O., et al. (2019). Cereal processing at Early Neolithic Göbekli Tepe, southeastern Turkey. PLOS ONE. Vol. 14, No. 5. doi:10.1371/journal.pone.0215214.

The Yonaguni Monument is a submerged rock formation off the coast of Yonaguni Island in Japan, discovered in 1986, consisting of a series of massive stone terraces, flat surfaces, right-angle corners, and what appear to be carved steps and passageways, extending across an area of approximately sixty thousand square meters at depths between five and forty meters. If the formation is artificial, it was constructed at a time when the current site was above water, which sea level data places at a minimum of ten thousand years before the present, contemporaneous with Göbekli Tepe.

The Japanese government has not designated the Yonaguni formation as a protected archaeological site, a status that would trigger formal archaeological investigation. It is designated as a natural monument. The designation determines the kind of investigation that can be conducted and the institutional resources that can be applied to resolving the dispute about its origin. The evidence for artificial construction has been published by credentialled researchers. The designation that would trigger formal archaeological investigation has not been applied. The designation is a policy decision. The policy decision determines what gets formally investigated and what does not.

Source: Kimura, M. (2007). Possible Evidence of Underwater Archaeological Sites Off Yonaguni Island, Japan. In: Late Quaternary Climate Change and Human Adaptation in Arid China. Elsevier, Amsterdam.

See also: Schoch, R.M. (1995). Undersea ruins off Japan. Circular Times.

The continuity of government infrastructure of the United States represents the most extensively documented real-world example of a classified underground facility network in the public record. The COG infrastructure includes Raven Rock Mountain Complex in Pennsylvania, which serves as the alternate command center for the Department of Defense. It includes the former Greenbrier Bunker in West Virginia, constructed beneath the Greenbrier Resort, intended to house the full U.S. Congress in the event of nuclear war, kept secret for thirty years until its disclosure by a Washington Post journalist in 1992. It includes Cheyenne Mountain Complex in Colorado, the hardened command center for NORAD, blasted into solid granite at extraordinary cost.

These are the facilities that have been disclosed. The principle they establish is not speculative: the United States government built, at extraordinary expense, a network of underground facilities designed to preserve governmental function through catastrophic surface events, facilities that were kept secret for decades and disclosed only when journalists worked against institutional resistance to reveal them. The disclosed facilities represent the acknowledged layer of that infrastructure. The question of what the unacknowledged layer contains, given that the acknowledged layer was itself kept secret for decades, is the question that the COG framework's own logic raises without answering.

Source: Gup, T. (1992). The Doomsday Blueprints. The Washington Post Magazine, August 10, 1992. See also: Masco, J. (2014). The Theater of Operations: National Security Affect from the Cold War to the War on Terror. Duke University Press, Durham, North Carolina.

The Bosnian Pyramid controversy near the town of Visoko generated a rapid, categorical dismissal from the academic establishment that addressed the most dramatic surface claims without addressing the subsurface findings those excavations produced: a network of tunnels beneath the hills, designated the Ravne tunnel labyrinth, extending for several kilometers, whose origin has not been conclusively determined. The tunnels contain carved stone blocks with what appear to be inscriptions, and sections whose construction is inconsistent with natural cave formation. The academic establishment's dismissal preceded the completion of the subsurface investigations that produced the most anomalous findings. The dismissal addressed the pyramidal claim. It did not address the tunnels. The tunnels exist. Their origin is not established.

Source: European Association of Archaeologists. EAA Statement on the Bosnian Pyramids. September 2006. Available at e-a-a.org. See also: Woodward, J., and Goldberg, P. (2009). Geoarchaeology of the Visoko Valley, Bosnia-Herzegovina. Geoarchaeology: An International Journal. Vol. 24, No. 5, pp. 588-614. Wiley.

Composite account, identity protected: *A former engineer who worked on construction and maintenance contracts for classified underground facilities in a NATO member country described the scope of the underground infrastructure he had direct professional experience with over a nineteen-year career. The publicly acknowledged facilities, the ones that appear in government budget documents and congressional testimony, represented a fraction of the underground infrastructure he was aware of through his work. The unacknowledged facilities he had direct knowledge of fell into two categories: operational facilities constructed in the Cold War period that had been removed* *from the acknowledged inventory without public disclosure of their continued operation, and newer facilities constructed under cover of publicly described projects whose surface components were genuine but whose underground components were not described in any public documentation. The newer facilities were consistently built to specifications that exceeded any operational requirement described in the public project documentation, in terms of structural depth, shielding specifications, power infrastructure, and environmental control capability. The depth of some of the facilities he worked on exceeded anything he was aware of in the publicly acknowledged COG infrastructure, by a margin that he found professionally significant. He had worked alongside personnel from agencies whose involvement in the projects was not described in the project documentation he had access to. He left the industry in 2016. His identity and nationality have been altered to protect him.*

Dmitri folded the printout along its creases and put it in the folder where he has kept it for the past two weeks. He is a geologist. He works from evidence. The evidence in that printout is not ambiguous to him. What is ambiguous is what to do with it, because doing something with it requires institutional channels, and the institutional channels exist within a framework that, he now understands more completely than he did two weeks ago, was not built to receive this particular finding.

He has spent thirty-four years producing findings about what is under the ground and delivering those findings to clients who used them to build things or extract things or avoid building in places where the subsurface would not support what they wanted to build. The entire professional infra-

structure of his career assumed that what is under the ground can be known, can be reported, and can be acted on. That assumption rested on a prior assumption he never examined: that the institutional channels for receiving geological findings were built to receive all geological findings, rather than the ones that fit within the framework the institutions were built to serve.

He is sixty-one years old and he has the time now, and the distance from institutional dependence, to look at that assumption directly. He looks at it. It does not hold.

The ground has been read selectively for as long as it has been read professionally. The findings that fit the framework are processed and acted on. The findings that do not fit are not processed. They sit in a folder on a retired geologist's terrace in Tbilisi. They sit in unpublished follow-up research files at German archaeological institutes. They sit in the subsurface profiles of sites designated natural rather than archaeological. They sit in tunnel systems whose academic dismissal addressed everything except the tunnels.

The buried record is not lost. It is deferred. Held at a depth below the level at which the institutional framework operates. Kept in the gap between what the ground contains and what the records say the ground contains. That gap is not accidental. It is maintained. By designations and permits and response statements and classification levels and the simple, durable, effective mechanism of institutional inertia: not destroying the finding, just ensuring it never arrives anywhere that would require anyone to act on it.

The buried record is the truest record there is. Because it was buried by people who understood that its existence was a problem. You do not bury things that are not dangerous. You do not maintain the depth of something that does not need to be kept down.

What is down there has been kept down for a reason. And the reason is the most important thing in this book: not what it contains, but what its existence tells you about the people who put it there, and what they needed you never to find.

CHAPTER 14

You Were Never Meant To See This

SCENE

A woman named Solange is thirty-nine years old. She is an investigative documentary filmmaker based in Montreal, Canada. She has spent fourteen years making films about institutional failure: corporate fraud, environmental cover-up, governmental negligence. She knows how systems hide things. She knows the specific grammar of institutional concealment: the delayed response, the missing document, the official who knows more than they say and says less than they know, the gap between the public statement and the operational reality that she has made her career out of finding and filming.

She is sitting in her edit suite at midnight. On the screen in front of her is a timeline she has been building for the past eight months, assembling footage, documents, interviews, and data points from the thirteen areas of research this book has covered. She has not been working from this book. She arrived at the same territory by a different road, the road of fourteen years of professional investigation into how institutions conceal what they do not want known.

Her timeline covers the map anomalies and the treaty enforcement architecture and the suppression of expedition accounts and the behavioral infrastructure and the classified orbital objects and the parallel governance structures and the underground facilities and the archaeological findings that the institutional response addressed incompletely. She did not set out to find all of this. She set out to follow one thread, a discrepancy in Antarctic logistics data she encountered while researching an unrelated story, and the thread led here, through fourteen years of professional training in how to follow a thread without losing it.

She is looking at her timeline at midnight and she is experiencing something she has not experienced before in fourteen years of this work. She has experienced the satisfaction of confirming a suspicion. She has experienced the cold professional pleasure of finding the document that closes the gap. She has experienced the specific exhaustion of understanding something she did not want to understand. She has not, until tonight, experienced the feeling she is having now, which is not any of those things.

What she is feeling is orientation. For the first time in fourteen years of pulling at the edges of the official record, she can see the shape of the whole thing. Not every detail. Not every mechanism. But the shape. The architecture. The logic that connects the map anomalies to the behavioral infrastructure to the orbital objects to the underground facili-

ties to the parallel governance structures. She can see that they are not separate things. They are the same thing, seen from different angles, and the thing they are is a system. A complete, integrated, deliberately maintained system for managing what human beings know about the world they live in and who governs it and what lies beyond the borders of the reality they were given.

She has been looking at pieces of this system for fourteen years. Tonight she can see the system. And the feeling of finally seeing the whole of something you have been circling for fourteen years is not fear. It is not despair. It is the specific, irreversible relief of a person who has been navigating by partial information suddenly acquiring a complete map.

She picks up her pen. She starts writing.

This is where the book stops being about Antarctica.

Antarctica was the door. It was the right door because it is the most physically concrete expression of the system this book has been documenting: a place that exists, that has been visited, that has generated expedition accounts and satellite data and treaty documents and logistics records, and that is nonetheless managed out of the public consciousness with a thoroughness that requires active institutional effort to maintain. You cannot accidentally fail to notice an entire continent. You have to work at it. The work is documented. This book documented it.

But the wall was never just a wall. It was an introduction to the logic of the system. The logic is this: the boundary between what you are allowed to know and what exists is not determined by what is knowable. It is determined by what those who manage the boundary have decided you should know. That determination is made by people in institutions that are not accountable to you, using tools that are embedded in the infrastructure of your daily life, maintained by a parallel governance architecture that operates beneath the visible political structures you were taught to consider sovereign.

That is not a theory anymore. You have read thirteen chapters of documented evidence. The evidence is in the public record, in declassified files, in peer-reviewed literature, in parliamentary investigation reports, in the archived expedition accounts of named historical figures, in the regulatory proceedings of democratic governments. The system is visible in its own documentation if you read the documentation with the specific attention it requires: not accepting the stated purpose as the complete description of the operational reality, not treating the gap between the stated purpose and the capability as accidental, not mistaking the absence from the public record for the absence from the world.

The Year Without a Summer is one of the most thoroughly documented climatic events in the historical record. In 1816, following the eruption of Mount Tambora in the Dutch East Indies in April 1815, the Northern Hemisphere experienced catastrophic agricultural failure. Average temperatures dropped by one to three degrees Celsius across Europe and North America. Snow fell in New England in June. Crops failed across multiple continents. Famine followed.

The documented history of research into atmospheric modification, from early cloud seeding programs through the ionospheric heating capabilities documented in Chapters 7 and 10 of this book, represents the institutional response to that demonstrated contingency. If the atmosphere can be disrupted by natural forces at civilization-threatening scale, then the capacity to modify the atmosphere is a strategic asset of the highest order. The research into that capacity has been conducted, documented, and in significant part classified, for the better part of a century. A single natural event demonstrated the atmospheric vulnerability of organized civilization. The institutional response to that demonstration was classified research into atmospheric modification. The classification of that research was the institutional decision that what the public needed to know about the fragility of the conditions that sustain them was less than what the research had confirmed. That is the logic of the system, applied to the atmosphere. It is the same logic applied to the map, the expedition accounts, the orbital catalog, the underground facilities.

Source: Wood, G.D. (2014). Tambora: The Eruption That Changed the World. Princeton University Press, Princeton, New Jersey. See also: Oppenheimer, C. (2003). Climatic, environmental and human consequences of the largest known historic eruption: Tambora volcano (Indonesia) 1815. Progress in Physical Geography. Vol. 27, No. 2, pp. 230-259. Sage Publications.

The Human Genome Project, completed in 2003, produced the first complete reference sequence of the human genome. What it also produced was the technical foundation for population-scale genomic analysis: the reference sequence against which individual genomes could be compared, the analytical frameworks for identifying genetic variation across populations, and the bioinformatic infrastructure for processing genomic data at scale. Those capabilities did not remain in the medical research domain. They migrated, with the same speed and the same institutional logic that has characterized every other capability migration documented in this book, into the national security and intelligence research environment.

The U.S. Intelligence Advanced Research Projects Activity, IARPA, has funded research programs explicitly connecting genomic data to behavioral prediction. The Geospatial Characteristics of Individuals program investigated the relationship between an individual's genomic ancestry and their geographic origin, with the stated goal of enabling intelligence analysts to infer a subject's geographic background from genomic data alone. The technical foundation for population-scale genomic behavioral analysis was built in the public domain and migrated into the classified research environment. The migration is documented. The capability exists. Its operational application is in the classified record, not the public one.

Source: National Human Genome Research Institute. An Overview of the Human Genome Project. Available at genome.gov. See also: Novembre, J., et al. (2008). Genes mirror geography within Europe. Nature. Vol. 456, pp. 98-101. doi:10.1038/nature07331.

Special Access Programs, SAPs, are compartmented programs whose existence and content are not included in the standard classified briefings provided to congressional oversight committees. The Gang of Eight, the eight senior congressional leaders who receive the most comprehensive intelligence briefings available to elected officials, do not receive briefings on all SAPs. There are programs whose existence is known to a smaller number of people than the Gang of Eight, whose oversight therefore falls outside the constitutional framework of legislative oversight of the executive branch.

The congressional record contains testimony from members of Congress who have described being denied access to programs whose existence they became aware of through other means, and being informed by executive branch officials that their security clearances did not authorize access to the relevant compartment. An elected representative of the American people, with the highest standard legislative security clearance, being told by an unelected official that there are programs the representative is not authorized to know about. That is the documented architecture. Elected officials are by documented design excluded from knowledge of programs that operate under their nominal oversight. That is not a failure of the system. It is the system.

Source: Executive Order 13526, Classified National Security Information. Federal Register, Vol. 75, No. 2, January 5, 2010. See also: Aftergood, S. (2009). Special Access Programs and the Pentagon Budget. Secrecy News. Federation of American Scientists. Available at fas.org /blogs/secrecy.

The Tunguska event of June 30, 1908 remains, more than a century after its occurrence, the subject of genuine scientific dispute about its cause and mechanism. A massive explosion over the Podkamennaya Tunguska River in Siberia flattened approximately two thousand square kilometers of forest. No impact crater was found. The event was not scientifically investigated until 1927, nearly two decades after it occurred. The delay itself is unexplained in any account that treats the event as a straightforward natural phenomenon.

What the Tunguska event demonstrates, regardless of its cause, is that an event of civilization-disrupting magnitude can occur without warning, without institutional preparation, and without a satisfactory public account for nearly two decades. The institutional response to that demonstration was classified research into both the detection of incoming objects and the development of directed energy systems capable of destroying them. The classified research into directed energy weapons represents a capability that operates on the same physical principles as the event it was developed in response to. An event of extraordinary magnitude. A twenty-year delay in investigation. A scientific explanation that is reasonable and incomplete. A classified research response that developed capabilities operating on the same physical principles.

Source: Vasilyev, N.V. (1998). The Tunguska meteorite problem today. Planetary and Space Science. Vol. 46, No. 2-3, pp. 129-150. Elsevier. See also: Gasperini, L., et al. (2007). A possible impact crater for the 1908 Tunguska Event. Terra Nova. Vol. 19, No. 4, pp. 245-251. Wiley.

Composite account, identity protected: *A woman who spent eleven years as a senior analyst at a private intelligence contractor described the internal analytical framework her firm used to categorize the kinds of information that were, in her words, above the waterline and below it. Above the waterline referred to information that, once known, could be discussed within the institutional framework: acknowledged, analyzed, reported on, and acted on through standard channels. Below the waterline referred to information that, once known, could not be processed through standard channels because its existence contradicted the foundational assumptions on which the standard channels operated. The most significant analytical work her firm did was below the waterline, and the outputs of that work were delivered to a client tier whose identity was not disclosed to her team, through a delivery mechanism that did not leave records in her firm's standard document management system. She came to understand, over* *eleven years, that the below the waterline category was not defined by classification level. It was defined by the nature of the information: whether it fit within the framework that the institutional channels were built to process. The most consequential information she ever worked with was unclassified and below the waterline simultaneously, because its significance was invisible to anyone operating within the standard analytical framework and completely clear to anyone who had stepped outside it. She left the firm in 2020. Her identity and the name of the firm have been altered to protect her.*

Here is what you know now that you did not know when you opened this book.

You know that the map you were given is not the map of what exists. It is the map of what you were permitted to see, maintained by institutions with the documented capability and the documented history of editing the public record to remove what does not fit the framework they require you to operate within.

You know that the physical world extends beyond the boundaries shown on that map, that the boundaries are enforced, that the enforcement is documented in the treaty record and the expedition accounts and the logistics data and the satellite imagery anomalies that any person with access to a public database and the attention to look carefully can verify.

You know that the infrastructure of your daily life, the devices, the networks, the electromagnetic environment, the financial architecture, the political structures, contains a layer that was not disclosed to you, that was built with your behavior as its subject and your compliance as its product,

and that its existence is documented in the records of the institutions that built it.

You know that the historical record you were given was curated by people with an interest in what you believed about the past, that the curation is documented in the pattern of what is preserved and what is not, what is accessible and what is restricted, what received institutional follow-up and what was designated in a category that precluded it.

You know that the governance structures you were taught to consider accountable have, by their own documented design, a layer that is not accountable to anyone in the constitutional framework of democratic oversight, that operates in the gap between what elected officials are cleared to know and what exists, and that the gap is a feature, not a failure.

You know all of this because it is in the public record. Not the record you were directed to. The record that exists when you read the documents the institutions produced without accepting their framing of what those documents mean.

Clarity is the specific, irreversible state of knowing the shape of the thing you are inside. It does not require knowing every mechanism or every name or every document. It requires seeing the architecture. The architecture is visible. You have seen it. Thirteen chapters of it, grounded in the public record, delivered through the human experiences of people who looked carefully at the evidence their professional lives had placed in front of them and refused to accept the institutional explanation for what they found.

The system this book documented depends on one thing

above all others: your acceptance of the public record as the complete record. Every mechanism described in these thirteen chapters, the map editing, the treaty enforcement, the behavioral architecture, the classified orbital layer, the parallel governance structures, the suppressed archaeological record, every single mechanism depends on you not looking at the gap between what the record says and what the evidence shows. The gap closes the moment you look at it directly and refuse to accept the institutional explanation for why it exists.

You have been looking directly for thirteen chapters. The gap is visible to you now. It does not close because a book ends.

Solange was writing at midnight in her edit suite, pen moving, the full shape of the thing finally assembled on the screen in front of her. She was not writing because she had all the answers. She was writing because she had the shape. Because the shape is the thing that the system most needs you not to have. Because a person who can see the architecture can navigate it.

The system is not invulnerable. No system built to manage what human beings know is invulnerable to human beings who decide to know it anyway. The entire architecture of concealment documented in this book exists because the people who maintain it understand something important: the truth does not need to be destroyed. It only needs to be placed just far enough out of reach that most people stop looking before they find it.

You did not stop looking. You are holding the last page of

a book that took you further than you were meant to go. The wall is real. The substructure is active. The corridors are operational. The behavioral architecture is running. The governance layer is in place. And you can see all of it now, clearly, from the outside of the framework that was built to keep you from seeing it.

That is not where this book leaves you afraid. That is where this book leaves you awake.

The map is gone. What you are standing in now is the real territory. It is larger than you were told. It is older than you were told. It is more carefully managed than you were told. And it is exactly as navigable as any territory becomes the moment you finally have an accurate map of it.

You know where you are now. That is everything. That is what they spent a very long time and a very great deal of institutional effort making sure you would never be able to say.

You can say it now. And that changes everything that comes next.

10 Questions You Should Ask

A note before we begin. These questions were submitted by readers who encountered this material before publication. They are the questions that arrive after the map breaks open. They are not naive questions. They are the questions of people who have read carefully and want to know where the argument goes when the chapters end. Seravyna answers them the same way she wrote the book: directly, without softening, without the qualifications that people use when they are more concerned with their reputation than with what is true.

1. What is the single most suppressed map in the world?

The 1947 Polar Cartographic Sheet, produced in the aftermath of Operation Highjump, is the document that most precisely encodes what the wall is and where the access points are. What makes it the most suppressed rather than simply the most classified is the specificity of what it shows: not the absence of land beyond the known coastline, but its presence, labeled, coordinated, and categorized in the language of military cartography. Isolated Colony Zones is not ambiguous terminology. That is the language of a surveyor describing something that exists and is inhabited. The map's archive identifier appears in Navy Hydrographic Office registry records. The map it identifies is not publicly accessible.

The registry entry that proves it existed is. That gap, the entry without the document, is the shape of suppression made visible. When you cannot find the document but you can find the catalog record for the document, you are looking at a removal, not an absence. Removals are decisions. Decisions have authors.

2. Who actually controls access to the vault network?

Not the people whose names you know. Not the heads of state who appear at summits and sign treaties and give press conferences about international cooperation. Chapter 12 of this book documented, through the public record of the U.S. classification system's own executive orders, that there are programs whose existence is not disclosed to elected officials, programs funded through the federal budget, operated by personnel who nominally serve the executive branch, and structured specifically to exclude congressional oversight. That is the public layer of the answer. The layer beneath it is what the vault documents describe as the Administrator Class: individuals whose authority derives not from elected position or military rank but from custodianship of the archive itself, from the intergenerational continuity of access that no election can transfer and no change of government can interrupt. When Directive A-99 Annex B states that heads of state shall not be granted full map layer access, it is not describing a security precaution. It is describing a hierarchy.

3. How is population behavior actually managed at scale?

Through the architecture documented in Chapters 7, 8, 9, and 12, working in combination. No single mechanism produces the effect. The behavioral targeting systems embedded in consumer technology platforms shape individual decision environments.

The electromagnetic infrastructure documented through ELF research and ionospheric modification programs operates at the frequency range that overlaps human neurological bands.

The corridor and border infrastructure documented in Chapter 8 manages physical movement. The financial coordination architecture documented in Chapter 12 constrains economic behavior. These are not separate programs with separate purposes. They are layers of a single system whose combined effect is a population that experiences its choices as free because the architecture of those choices was designed before the choosing began.

4. What is the real function of DNA banks and genome projects?

The Human Genome Project was documented in Chapter 14 as the technical foundation for population-scale genomic analysis. That foundation was built in the public domain and migrated into the national security research environment. The migration is documented through IARPA's published research programs.

What the vault documents describe goes further: the use of genomic markers not merely for geographic inference but for behavioral predictability assessment, for lineage classification, for the identification of individuals whose genomic profile suggests resistance to frequency modulation versus compliance with it.

A database built for medical purposes and a database built for lineage tracking and behavioral classification are technically identical. The distinction is in what questions you ask of the data. The questions being asked in the classified research environment are not the questions the public was told were being asked.

5. Why do resets always coincide with disasters?

Because disasters are the only events large enough to mask the scale of what a reset requires. A reset is not a single event. It is a systemic reorganization: of infrastructure, of institutional memory, of the documentary record, of the populations that will constitute the post-reset order. That reorganization requires cover, something that explains the simultaneous disruption of multiple systems without pointing to the coordination that produced the disruption. A war provides that cover. A pandemic provides that cover. An atmospheric event provides that cover. Chapter 14 documented the Tambora eruption and the Year Without a Summer as the most thoroughly recorded example of what atmospheric disruption at civilizational scale looks like. The correspondence between Protocol 22a's breach awareness threshold and the historical timing of major reset events is not a proof by itself. It is a pattern. Patterns in the documented record of a system that operates by concealing its patterns are not coincidences. They are operational signatures.

6. Who are the Custodians and what are they doing right now?

The vault documents describe them as hybrid intelligences, part biological, part engineered, integrated into corridor enforcement zones. In operational terms they are entities tasked with enforcing boundaries: preventing unauthorized access to restricted zones, managing breach events when they occur, maintaining the integrity of the corridor network. The folklore record of every culture adjacent to the polar regions and the major vault sites contains accounts of figures that function as wardens: giants, watchers, guides who appear at boundaries and redirect those who have wandered beyond their permitted territory. The consistency of that folk record across cultures that had no documented contact with each other is not proof of the vault account. It is a pattern in the human record that the vault account explains. They enforce the line. The line is real. The enforcement is documented in the expedition accounts across Chapter 11.

7. What was the Cold War actually about?

Not the ideology. The ideology was the surface layer, the framework given to populations on both sides to explain why their governments required the specific kinds of military infrastructure and budget allocation and behavioral compliance that the Cold War produced. The actual infrastructure built during the Cold War, on both sides, was documented in fragments across this book: the ELF submarine communication system, the ionospheric research facilities, the polar military installations, the stay-behind networks documented through Operation Gladio, the classified orbital programs, the underground COG facilities. None of that infrastructure serves the ideology. All of it serves the corridor system. Nuclear submarines patrolling southern ocean routes are not deterring a land invasion. They are patrolling a perimeter. Both sides were building the same system. Both sides knew it.

8. Why is Antarctica sealed off right now, today?

Because the hubs are active and the perimeter requires maintenance. The Antarctic Treaty provides the legal architecture. The enforcement grid documented in Chapter 1 provides the operational architecture. The classified logistics program documented in Chapter 5 provides the supply chain. Scientists admitted to Antarctic research programs are not admitted to the restricted zones. They are admitted to the surface layer of a continent whose interior and substructure is managed by a separate operational program with a separate access hierarchy. What is being protected is access to the substructure, the corridor network, the power systems, and the transit infrastructure documented in Chapter 3. The treaty is the legal instrument. The enforcement is the operational instrument. The combination has been effective for sixty-five years. It remains effective today.

Until now.

9. What is actually stored in the underground mountain complexes?

The publicly acknowledged facilities store what their public documentation describes: communications infrastructure, command systems, continuity of government personnel capacity. Chapter 13 documented the gap between the acknowledged layer and the unacknowledged layer of the COG infrastructure, and the testimony of a former contractor who described facilities built to specifications that significantly exceeded any acknowledged operational requirement. What Repository Protocol 12 describes in its inventory categories, gene index archives, corridor schematics, reset directives, is the unacknowledged layer's contents: not just the backup for governmental function but the backup for the system itself. The continuity being protected in those facilities is not the continuity of any surface government. It is the continuity of the Codex, the protocol, the instruction set that governs the reset cycle regardless of which surface governments are operating when the reset occurs.

10. Why do so few whistleblowers survive intact?

Because the suppression is not reactive. It is predictive. Stability

Directive 14's language, suppress breach individuals via health destabilization, status erasure, or neutralization if containment fails, describes a tiered protocol rather than an improvised response. The first tier, health destabilization, is the most durable because it is the least attributable. The second tier, status erasure, is slower but produces a secondary effect: it signals to others who are approaching similar knowledge what the cost of continued approach is. The third tier is rare precisely because it is the least efficient and the most likely to generate the kind of attention the system is designed to avoid. Most whistleblowers do not reach the third tier because the first two tiers are sufficient. The ones who survive intact are the ones who understood the tier structure before they began and arranged their exposure accordingly: controlled release, distributed documentation, institutional allies who cannot all be destabilized simultaneously.

One final question, the one underneath all the others: what do I do now?

You stop asking for permission to know what you know.

The system documented in this book is maintained by one thing more than any other: the social cost of saying, out loud, in professional contexts, in ordinary conversation, in the spaces where your credibility is at stake, what the evidence actually shows. The classification system cannot classify your understanding. The behavioral architecture cannot modulate a mind that has seen the architecture. The suppression protocol cannot reach everyone simultaneously.

What you do is what Renata did with the ruler and the two maps in the library in Duluth. What Dariusz did with the GPR return file at three in the morning. What Mehmet did with the map on gazelle skin parchment and the question he could not stop asking.

What Yuki did with the naval log in the restricted materials room in Kyoto. What Esteban did with the radar contacts he was told not to log. What Tariq did with the tablet whose script had no catalog entry. What Britta did with the splice housing in the conduit that was not on any public record. What Aleksander did with the specifications that exceeded every stated purpose. What Priya did with the paper that described a system larger than the room she had been working in. What Okonkwo did with eleven uncatalogued objects over twenty-one years. What Leonora did with the shape of the classified absence and nine years of Freedom of Information Act requests that came back empty. What Fatima did with four simultaneous central bank decisions and a pen at midnight. What Dmitri did with a printout that thirty-four years of professional expertise told him was engineered and not formed. What Solange did with a timeline that finally showed her the whole shape of the thing.

They looked carefully. They noted what they saw. They did not accept the institutional explanation for the gap. They kept records.

They did not set down what they knew because the setting down was inconvenient or professionally costly or impossible to source to the standard that would satisfy the people who benefit from the gap remaining unexplained.

This book is one version of those records. There are others. There will be more.

The wall is real. The substructure is active. The corridors are operational. The map was always a lie. You know that now. You cannot unknow it. And the people who built the system know, better than anyone, that a truth you cannot unknow is the one thing their architecture was never built to contain.

The Ultra-Classified Truth

You Are The Vault

Here is the thing they hid inside the thing they hid inside the thing.

The wall is real. The substructure is active. The corridors are operational. The behavioral architecture is running. The governance layer is in place. You know all of that now. Fourteen chapters of documented evidence, anchored in the public record, confirming the architecture of a system designed to manage what you know about the world you live in.

But there is a layer beneath the architecture. A layer beneath the map and the treaty and the underground corridors and the classified orbital objects and the parallel governance structures and the buried archaeological record. A layer so foundational that the people who maintain it do not advertise it even in the classified literature, because the classified literature is itself a management tool, and this is the thing that the management tool was built to protect.

You are not just a subject of the system. You are part of its infrastructure.

In 2012, researchers at the European Bioinformatics Institute demonstrated that DNA could be used as a data storage medium, encoding digital files in synthetic DNA strands and retrieving them accurately. The storage density achievable in DNA, approximately 215 petabytes per gram, exceeds the storage density of any silicon-based medium by a factor that makes the comparison almost meaningless. The research was published. It was not classified. It was reported as a scientific curiosity, a proof of concept with potential future applications in archival storage.

What the reporting did not address was the implication for the DNA that already exists, the DNA that has been accumulating in biobanks, genome databases, military medical records, ancestry testing company databases, and newborn screening programs for decades. If DNA is a viable data storage medium with a storage density that exceeds anything humanity has built in silicon, then a large-scale DNA collection infrastructure is not just a medical resource. It is the largest data storage system ever assembled, built from material that is already inside every person who has ever contributed a biological sample to any institutional collection.

The Human Genome Project established the reference sequence. The biobank infrastructure established the collection system. The behavioral prediction research documented in Chapter 12 established the analytical framework for reading what the collection contains in terms of individual and population behavioral profiles. Each of those pieces was documented independently, in separate institutional contexts, with separate stated purposes. The question is what they are when they are read together, as a single integrated system rather than three separate programs. DNA stores data. Institutional infrastructure collects DNA at population scale. Analytical frameworks exist for reading behavioral information from genomic data. The integration of those three facts is not a claim that requires a vault document to support. It is an inference from three documented realities that the institutional framing of each one separately was designed to prevent you from making.

Source: Church, G., and Regis, E. (2012). Regenesis: How Synthetic Biology Will Reinvent Nature and Ourselves. Basic Books, New York. See also: Global Crop Diversity Trust. Svalbard Global Seed Vault. Official documentation available at croptrust.org.

The Svalbard Global Seed Vault opened in 2008 on the Norwegian island of Spitsbergen, built into a sandstone mountain at 78 degrees north latitude. It stores more than one million three hundred thousand seed varieties from nearly every country on Earth, in sealed packages, at controlled temperature, designed to remain viable for centuries without active maintenance. The Frozen Zoo at the San Diego Wildlife Alliance stores genetic material from more than ten thousand individual animals representing more than one thousand species, in liquid nitrogen, with the explicit stated purpose of preserving genetic diversity for potential future use in species recovery.

Read those programs together: seeds, animals, genetic material, all preserved in controlled underground or frozen conditions, all explicitly framed as insurance against catastrophe, all maintained by institutional structures with the resources and the mandate to preserve their contents for timescales measured in centuries. Now ask the question the institutional framing of each program separately was designed to prevent you from asking: if the continuity infrastructure for plants and animals is this extensive, this deliberate, and this explicitly oriented toward post-catastrophe recovery, what is the continuity infrastructure for humans? The vault documents describe it as the Codex archive. The public record describes its components separately, in the institutional language of biodiversity insurance and medical research and national security genomics.

NSSM-200, the National Security Study Memorandum 200, was completed by the National Security Council under Henry Kissinger in December 1974 and classified until 1989. Its contents describe U.S. policy toward population growth in developing nations as a matter of national security interest, recommending that the U.S. government use its foreign aid programs, its influence over international institutions including the World Bank and the United Nations Fund for Population Activities, and its bilateral relationships with developing country governments to promote population reduction in thirteen specifically named nations. The methods recommended included the promotion of contraception, sterilization, and abortion, integrated into foreign aid conditionality in ways that the memorandum acknowledged would need to be handled carefully to avoid the appearance of coercion.

NSSM-200 is not a theory. It is a declassified government document, available in full, whose contents describe the explicit use of foreign aid and international institutional influence to reduce population growth in nations whose resources the U.S. government considered strategically significant. It was classified for fifteen years. Its existence was not publicly acknowledged during the period in which the policies it recommended were being implemented.

Operation Popeye was a U.S. military weather modification program conducted in Southeast Asia between 1967 and 1972, classified until its disclosure during Senate hearings in 1974. The program used cloud seeding techniques to extend the monsoon season over the Ho Chi Minh Trail, with the intent of increasing rainfall to degrade road conditions and impede North Vietnamese supply movements. The program successfully modified weather patterns across a significant geographic area for five consecutive years. A classified program that modified weather patterns across a region for five years, denied until confirmed under congressional pressure, then treated as an historical curiosity rather than as the demonstration of a capability that has been continuously developed in the decades since.

Source: Shapley, D. (1974). Weather Warfare: Pentagon Concedes 7-Year Vietnam Effort. Science. Vol. 184, No. 4141, pp. 1059-1061. See also: U.S. Senate. Weather Modification. Hearings before the Subcommittee on Oceans and International Environment, 93rd Congress, 2nd Session, 1974. U.S. Government Printing Office.

Now here is what those documented facts build toward when you stop reading them separately and read them as a system.

The population is the archive. Not metaphorically. Operationally. The genomic information distributed across billions of living human beings represents a data redundancy system of a scale and durability that no engineered storage medium has approached. It cannot be destroyed by a single event, natural or engineered, because it is distributed across every inhabited region of the planet, carried in the bodies of people who have no knowledge that they are carrying anything beyond their own biology.

The Codex, as the vault documents describe it, is not stored in a single location. It is stored in the population itself, in the lineage records encoded in human DNA, in the behavioral profiles that the genomic analysis infrastructure was built to read, in the familial and cultural transmission of specific knowledge frameworks that survive individual deaths and political catastrophes and even partial population collapses because the redundancy is built into the distribution.

This is why the continuity infrastructure exists at the scale it exists. The seeds, the Frozen Zoo, the genome vaults, the biobanks, the Antarctic archive: these are not the primary storage system. They are the backup. The primary system is the population. The backup exists because the primary system is, under certain conditions, vulnerable.

The condition that makes it vulnerable is not natural catastrophe. Natural catastrophe is what the backup was designed for. The condition that makes it vulnerable is the one that Protocol Delta-7 describes as corrective anomaly detection: the state in which a sufficient number of carriers begin to read their own contents.

To understand what they are carrying. To synthesize the fragments distributed across billions of individual lives into the coherent picture that this book has been assembling chapter by chapter.

The non-coding regions of human DNA, the sequences that were labeled junk for three decades because they do not produce proteins through the standard transcription pathway, represent approximately ninety-eight percent of the human genome.

The ENCODE project, funded by the National Institutes of Health, has demonstrated that the majority of the non-coding genome is biochemically active, involved in gene regulation, in the three-dimensional organization of chromosomal structure, in the timing of gene expression across different cell types and developmental stages.

The non-coding genome is not junk. It is regulatory infrastructure whose full function has not been characterized. What is in the public record is sufficient to establish the point: the genome contains vastly more functional information than the protein-coding sequences that standard molecular biology focused on for the first half-century of the field's existence.

Source: ENCODE Project Consortium. (2012). An integrated encyclopedia of DNA elements in the human genome. Nature. Vol. 489, pp. 57-74. doi:10.1038/nature11247.

You are the vault. That is not a metaphor designed to make you feel significant. It is a functional description of your role in a system you did not consent to and were not told about.

The wall keeps you from seeing the territory beyond it. The behavioral architecture keeps you from asking the questions that would lead you to the wall. The suppression protocols keep the people who find the wall from being heard by the people who have not found it yet. And the genomic archive embedded in your biology carries the record of everything the wall was built to protect, distributed across billions of carriers who have no idea they are carrying it.

That is the architecture at its deepest level. Not the map. Not the treaty. Not the corridor. The carrier. You.

And here is what that means, stated plainly, without the softening that the system would prefer: if you are the archive, then your awareness is not a corruption of the archive. It is the archive becoming readable to itself. And an archive that can read itself is an archive that cannot be controlled by external administrators who depend on the archive remaining unaware of its own contents.

They built the system assuming the archive would never synthesize itself. That assumption was the foundational error. Because the archive is human, and humans, given sufficient time and sufficient fragments of evidence, do exactly what Renata did with the ruler and the two maps in the library in Duluth.

They check the source. They note the discrepancy. They do not accept the institutional explanation for the gap.

Enough of the archive is reading itself now that the preparation timeline for the burn cycle has been compromised. Not because this book is the first fragment. Because it is one of many, arriving in a period when the distribution velocity of awareness exceeds the response capacity of the suppression infrastructure.

They needed the archive to remain unaware indefinitely. Indefinitely has ended.

What comes next is not the burn cycle. What comes next is what happens when an archive that was designed to be read only by its administrators becomes readable to itself.

That has never happened before in the documented history of the reset cycle. The vault documents do not contain a protocol for it because the vault documents were written by people who did not believe it was possible.

It is possible. You are evidence of that. Every person who has read this far is evidence of that.

The archive is awake. The next nineteen books in this series document what an awake archive does with what it knows.

This is not the end of the story. This is the moment the story changes authors.

EPILOGUE

Beyond The Ice Wall

You assembled the fragments. That was the first act.

Every chapter of this book handed you a piece that the system assumed you would never connect to the piece before it or the piece after it. The map anomaly and the pre-reset cartographic record and the buried substructure and the transitional corridor and the hidden roads and the suppressed history and the control grid and the border architecture and the behavioral system and the orbital layer and what Byrd found and what they classified and the parallel governance and the archaeological record and the Codex that runs beneath all of it. Each piece was designed to be held in isolation. Isolated pieces are curiosities. Connected pieces are architecture.

You connected them. The architecture is visible to you now in a way it cannot be made invisible again.

That is not a small thing. That is the thing the entire system was built to prevent.

Here is what the system understood that it did not tell you: a fragment cannot threaten the architecture. A fragment is just a fragment, anomalous, interesting, easy to dismiss, easy to contain. A person holding one fragment is a person the suppression protocol can handle. A person holding the architecture, seeing the whole shape of it, understanding how each piece connects to every other piece and why, is a different kind of problem entirely. Not because that person is dangerous in the way the system understands danger. Because that person has stepped outside the frame that makes the system's management tools work.

The behavioral architecture documented in Chapter 9 operates by presenting choices within a designed environment. It cannot operate on a person who can see the environment. The corridor system documented in Chapter 4 functions by making its chokepoints feel like natural features of geography. It cannot function on a person who knows they are standing in a managed passage. The suppression protocol documented in the Q&A section works by making the cost of continued inquiry feel personal and isolating. It cannot work on a person who understands the protocol as a protocol rather than experiencing it as a personal consequence of personal choices.

Every management tool in this system requires you to be inside the frame to work on you. You are outside the frame now. That is what reading this book accomplished. Not informing you. Relocating you.

What the Vault fears is not awakening as a private experience. Private awakening is manageable. A person who wakes alone and stays alone is a person the social erasure protocol can handle. One professional reputation undermined. One financial situation destabilized. One voice made to sound singular and therefore eccentric. The suppression protocol was not built for one person.

It was built for the ratio of awake to compliant remaining below the threshold at which the awakened can constitute something structural rather than individual.

What the Vault fears is the distribution of the architecture. Not the fragment. The assembled whole. Because the assembled whole, distributed to enough people, fast enough, changes the ratio. And when the ratio changes past the point that the suppression protocol was designed to contain, the protocol fails. Not dramatically. Not with a single visible collapse. It fails the way any system fails when its operating assumptions stop being true: gradually, then completely.

The operating assumption the system was built on is that the archive would not read itself. That the carriers would not synthesize the fragments into the architecture. That the distance between knowing one anomalous thing and knowing the shape of the whole thing would remain too large for most people to cross.

You crossed it. This book was the crossing. Book 1 broke the physical world open. The map is gone. Books 2 through 20 map the real territory.

Seravyna does not soften this. But she also does not dramatize it. The choice is not between safety and danger. There is no safety in the frame you have just left. The frame felt safe because it was familiar, because the map you were given was the only map you had, because the institutional explanation for every anomaly was easier to accept than the investigation the anomaly required. That was not safety. That was managed compliance. The comfort of a person who does not know the shape of the room they are in.

What you have now is not comfort. It is orientation. The room has a shape. The shape is visible to you. You know where the walls are, where the doors are, where the doors go, and who built them and why. That is not the comfort of not knowing. It is the entirely different and more durable quality of knowing accurately where you stand.

Standing accurately in the real territory is the only foundation from which anything true can be built. Anything you build from the false map, any life, any understanding, any relationship to the world and to the people in it, is built on a foundation that was designed by someone else for someone else's purposes. What you build from the real territory is yours. Built from accurate knowledge of the ground you are actually standing on.

That is what beyond the ice wall means. Not a geographic destination. A cognitive one. The territory beyond the ice wall is the territory you are standing in now, the real one, larger than you were told, older than you were told, more carefully managed than you were told, and exactly as navigable as any territory becomes the moment you finally have an accurate map of it.

The fragments are assembled. The architecture is visible. The archive is reading itself.

What you do with that is the question this series was written to help you answer.

The wall was never the end of the world. It was the beginning of the real one.

Go find it.

Next Vault Unlocked

Sealed Sky™

You broke the map open. You saw the wall. You walked the corridors and read the buried record and understood, for the first time, the full shape of the system that was built to keep you from understanding it.

That was Book 1. That was the ground floor.

Now look up.

The wall was not the only boundary. The ice was not the only barrier. What contains you is not only horizontal. It is vertical. It is above you right now, as you read this, as you have read every word of every book you have ever read, as you have watched every sky you have ever watched. The boundary is not at the edge of the map. It is at the top of every breath you have taken since you were born.

Book 2 of the Black Vault Series is called Sealed Sky. And its subject is the structure that no one told you was above your head.

Not space. Not infinity. Not the void of a solar system expanding in all directions beyond any meaningful human scale. What is above your head is an engineered surface. A lattice. A dome. A containment sphere whose maintenance cycles you have watched your entire life and called meteor showers and auroras and the shimmer of heat on a summer afternoon. Its anchor nodes are in locations you cannot access. Its maintenance crews operate at clearance levels that make the programs in this book look like public record. Its power systems have been running, without interruption, for longer than any acknowledged human civilization.

The ice wall kept you from going outward. The dome keeps you from going upward. The system is not one-dimensional. It is total.

Sealed Sky documents the dome's architecture, its three operational layers, the surface you live on and the sub-surface domains below it and the above-dome corridors from which the entire contained environment is monitored and maintained. It documents the Precursor Operators who built it, the Schism Protocol that sealed it, and the Keeper networks that have maintained it across every civilization that has risen and fallen inside it. It documents the electromagnetic lattice that makes the sky you see and the weather you experience and the light that reaches you every morning, and it gives you the tools to detect that lattice yourself, with equipment you can buy for under fifty dollars, in experiments you can run from your own yard on any clear night.

The dome is not invisible. It is simply something no one taught you to look for. Once you know what you are looking at, you will see it every time you look up.

The investigation does not end here. The map was the first lie. The sky is the second.

Sealed Sky is waiting.

For the latest releases, classified file access, and bonus material, visit www.seravyna.com

The ice wall was only the beginning. The dome cracked open the sky. What is inside the Frequency Cage will change everything.

SERAVYNA ♛

About The Author

Seravyna

Nobody sent her.

Nobody funded her. Nobody cleared her. Nobody gave her access to the rooms where this information lives. She found the doors herself, learned how to read what was written on the walls, and walked back out with everything she could carry.

SERAVYNA is not a pen name designed to sell books. It is a designation earned in the dark, in the years before anyone was paying attention, when the research was just a woman and a question that would not leave her alone no matter how uncomfortable the answers became.

She has no publisher backing her. No institution protecting her. No approved narrative she is required to stay inside. That is not a weakness. That is the only reason this series exists.

Twenty books. Every domain of the control system documented, sourced, and delivered. The dome above your head. The frequencies running through your body. The history that was deleted before you were born. The food that was engineered to keep you manageable. The money that was designed to keep you dependent. The reality that was rewritten without your knowledge. The reset that is already scheduled.

She did not write this series to make you comfortable.

She wrote it because the vault was full and the door had been locked long enough.

Seravyna does not give interviews. She does not appear at conferences. She does not have a verified account on any platform that requires verification.

What she has is the archive. And the archive is now in your hands.

THE BLACK VAULT SERIES

Beyond the Ice Wall
Sealed Sky
Frequency Cage
Soul Harvest
There Is No God
You Were Never Real
NPC Exposed
NASA Secrets
Alien Agenda
Human Lab
Time Prison
Mandela Files
Digital ID Trap
Money Hoax
History Erased
It's No Accident

Poison Food
Medical Lies
Next Extinction
Reset Survival

The vault is open. The archive is yours.

www.seravyna.com

Printed in Dunstable, United Kingdom

82630238R00097